TWO LIVES TWO WORLDS

TWO LIVES TWO WORLDS

an autobiography

SHEILA CHICHESTER

*What things soever ye desire, when ye pray,
believe that ye receive them, and ye shall
have them.   St. Mark's Gospel, XI. 24.*

HODDER AND STOUGHTON

Printed in Great Britain for Hodder and Stoughton Limited, St. Paul's House, Warwick Lane, London, E.C.4. by C. Tinling & Co. Ltd, London and Prescot.

For Francis, my guide and inspiration,
and for our son Giles, who has sailed
with us since he was seven and helped
us in all our projects.

Acknowledgments

My grateful thanks are due to Robin Denniston
who gave me a framework for the book, to
Elsie Herron without whose help and encouragement
it would never have been written, also
to Bill Beresford who
produced the title in
just three seconds.

ILLUSTRATIONS

facing page

Sheila, aged 4   32
Mother, Sheila and Kathleen   32
Sheila's prize-winning drawing   33
Wren House, Kensington Palace   48
Mother and author in Sheila's first car   48
Sheila in a tennis dress made by herself   49
With friends in the South of France   49
On Addis Ababa race-course   49
Sheila's original hat designs   64
Mobile canteen in the London Docks, 1939-45 War   65
9 St. James's Place, London[1]   65
Sheila and Francis on their wedding day   80
Sheila and Giles, The Fishing Cottage, Stitchcombe   80
The author's portraits of Francis and Miranda[1]   81
Sheila with the entrants before the first Single-Handed
    Race, 1960   96
Meeting Francis winning Single-Handed Trans-Atlantic
    Race[2]   96
Sheila at the start of her voyage across the Atlantic, 1960   97
At the party to celebrate Francis's election as "Yachtsman
    of the Year"[3]   97
On board *Gipsy Moth III* at Cape Cod, 1962[4]   112
Homecoming, Plymouth, 1962[5]   112
Launching *Gipsy Moth IV*, Gosport, 1966[6]   113
After the dedication of *Gipsy Moth IV* at Tower Pier,
    London   113
Sheila in *Gipsy Moth IV* leaves for Sydney Heads   128
Sheila greets Francis after his solo circumnavigation
    at speed[7]   128
In the Channel before being met by the Queen at
    Greenwich[8]   129
Gipsy Moth IV arrives at Greenwich Pier   129
The Queen welcoming Sheila at the Watergate,
    Greenwich[9]   144

facing page

The Lord Mayor and Lady Mayoress of London and
Lord Simon's grandson at Tower Pier, 7th July 1967[10]   144

Sheila escorted by Admiral of the Fleet, Earl Mountbatten
of Burma, at a banquet to commemorate Sir Francis
receiving the accolade[11]   145

KEY TO ACKNOWLEDGMENTS

[1]Donald Southern

[2]London Express News &
Feature Services

[3]Fox Photos Ltd

[4]Lockwood Studios, Cape Cod

[5]Associated Newspapers

[6]A. V. Swaebe

[7]Terry Spencer, courtesy *Life
Magazine* © Time Inc.

[8]Errol Bruce

[9]Central Press Photos Ltd

[10]Photographic News Agencies Ltd

[11]*Kentish Times*

FOREWORD

Life is full of surprises. I had never thought I should come into the public eye through wearing a red trouser suit, but apparently it caused a sensation that I should have appeared in one at the Knighting of Francis in July 1967.

On the occasion itself I was completely unaware of any unusual interest. The following day we had promised to open an exhibition near where *Gipsy Moth* was anchored. She had been towed into position in St. Catherine's Dock, and Francis, our son Giles and I went down there. When we arrived I found Press attention focussed on me because of the trouser suit at the Investiture. Now, this suit was ordered long before I knew the Queen was going to honour Francis in a special way. When I got home from Australia, I thought I'd better have a new trouser suit to wear for meeting Francis at Plymouth. Knowing he is fond of red, I struck out and had this colour, although it is not my favourite. I wore it at the Knighting because I was sailing—I was a member of the crew and had sailed all the way from Plymouth in *Gipsy Moth*. Next day I wore an ordinary dark print dress and coat because I wasn't sailing—and in any case women do like a change. Anyway, the Press went on crowding me until finally I said to the Editor of the *Sunday Times* who was with me: "Please tell them that I had permission to wear the trouser suit. The Palace knew what I was going to wear, and so did the Mansion House." Their faces fell. One doesn't mind criticism but they might have checked their facts. Even some of my older friends were unkind about it. But I was very happy on that great day, felt I was dressed correctly and gave no further thought to the matter.

Later on I had a letter from Caroline Travis, my goddaughter in Greece. "Hurrah for the red trouser suit," she wrote. Walking in the Park I began to see quite a number of these suits, so mine had been something of a trend-setter. This delighted me because of my lifelong interest in fashion. The Editor of *Queen* magazine told me, "With one act you have become a leader in fashion," and it is remarkable how interested people still are in what they call "the red trouser story". In New York recently I was dining with my husband's publisher, Jack Geoghegan. "Do you mind if I ask you something very personal?" he said. "What is the real inner story of the trouser suit?" When I told him, "May I dine out on that all this week?" he asked, and once again I was amazed at the interest.

Now, more than two years after the event, trouser suits are accepted wear. I have heard of a few restaurants foolish enough to turn away women in trousers, but on the whole in London and Paris women wear them when they feel like it. There are some very beautiful ones about; I think the girls look marvellous in them and that they're also flattering to the mature woman.

On that occasion I registered as the Woman in the Red Trouser Suit. Most people naturally think of me as the wife of a famous man. To myself I suppose I seem a kind of bridge, or channel of communication. Communication is a subject which has fascinated me all my life and it is one which will appear often in this book.

The means by which human beings get in touch with one another, the extent to which it is possible—in fact, communication of all kinds—I find a fascinating subject, and I have been thinking about this while I've been looking back over the past. It seems to me that communication, by which I mean the deepening of sympathy and understanding between people, is the essence of human life. Communication, too, between man and God, for though only the Saints can achieve a close relationship, the way is open to all. From my own personal experience, I know of the power of prayer and the possibility of healing in a miraculous way.

In the spring of 1958 when my husband was diagnosed as having lung cancer I had to put my beliefs to the test. It took more courage to question the opinion of an eminent surgeon than ever it called for to cross the Atlantic with Francis on the return trip from his triumphant Single-handed Solo Race. I knew that a diseased lung that had been cut out could never grow again, but that if it was left and treated, it had a chance to recover. My instinct tells me that healing is best done by natural methods and I believe in natural laws—a long-term process and a test of endurance and faith both for the doctor or priest and the patient.

The instant, mechanical means of communication, again, are

marvels I've reason to appreciate. If, for example, you can pick up what somebody is saying in a small yacht 5,000 miles away in the Atlantic, this is an astounding feat of communication. During Francis's voyage round the world in *Gipsy Moth IV*, I felt myself sailing with him mentally and physically; it was almost frightening really to be in such close touch. And over 29,000 miles of ocean passage, his adventure was shared by the public, men, women and children, and his position watched for week by week with tremendous interest. All this was done by means of twice weekly despatches sent by radio/telephone.

A rather wise friend of mine has said that communication has got ahead of man and that this is one of the problems of today. I think this is true; for better or worse, communication has developed phenomenally fast. Wars in what was once literally the Far East flash on to T.V. screens in one's comfortable sitting-room and the actuality arouses a world conscience. Perhaps this method of communication through mass media may yet be the means of saving races from fighting one another, or dying of starvation without those who are well-fed feeling that something must be done about it. In the old days these things happened and very few people in this country were aware of them at all.

You can fly to Australia now in under thirty hours and you can telephone in a minute, just dial and you get it, crystal clear. When we dug in our gardens as children, my sister and I, we always hoped to find Australia. We'd been told it was at the bottom of the earth and we firmly believed it. Today it seems almost as primitive as the people who thought the world was flat, and that when they got to the edge they'd just fall off. Most of us have moved on a great way at high speed since we were young. Particularly my generation, modern life is very cut off from natural elements. Man is creating an artificial world for himself, in which it is difficult to think clearly and keep one's balance. But the human frame is extraordinary in what it will stand up to, and the human spirit is strong. The great thing is to try to get soul and body working together in harmony. Living and working in London, I have a very strenuous, very happy life, discovering on my own doorstep things I'd have thought once that one must travel the world to find.

1

MY FATHER committed suicide when I was three days old. This must have been the most terrible thing for my mother, and in those days, of course, it was a frightful scandal. My paternal grandfather, who was a very rich man—he had made his fortune in Manchester as an engineer—had just bought Kirklington Hall, a mansion in Nottinghamshire. We lived at Belle Eau Park, one of the houses on the estate, and my father's death must have been a great blow to him socially. At any rate he wrote to my mother saying: "With Gerald's death all my responsibility to you and the children ceases." My poor mother! She had only about fifty pounds a year of her own at that time, left her by my great-grandmother Mary Ann Thurston, who was twenty-five years with Queen Victoria as head of the royal nurseries. Social Security was still far in the future, my mother was not trained in any profession (very few women were then) and in any case it would have been impossible for her to take a job with a baby of a few days old and another of eighteen months, my sister Kathleen. As for the scandal which must have made my grandfather want to wash his hands of us, thank goodness people are more tolerant these days. He did, however, give us a small allowance later.

Kathleen and I were never told what happened to my father and to the day of my mother's death she never knew that I knew. I felt I must go on acting it out since she did not want us told, but in fact the mystery was solved for me when I was eighteen. I was talking about it on a visit to Oxford when a friend of my current boy-friend came out with the answer. "Oh well," he said, "he committed suicide." So that was what the servants whispered about and why they used to call us "poor little Miss Kathleen and Sheila." My first reaction was relief; I had thought he was going to tell me I was illegitimate. This had haunted me for years. And then immediately I felt terribly sorry for my father, and for mother, who must have felt she'd failed him to let this happen. I rushed off and told my sister. Kathleen was furiously angry with me: "I wish you hadn't told me, I don't want to know anything about it."

Soon after the tragedy we moved to a charming house in Gloucestershire which is my earliest memory. The thing I remember best about my early childhood is the terrible grief I felt when our governess died. I was seven then. She was beautiful and I thought her a very romantic figure. I also remember my Welsh nanny, who was only with us two years but was a most vivid character. She's still alive and I am devoted to her. After our beloved governess died my sister and I had a series of others. We must have been so badly behaved that no-one would stay. At any rate when I was eleven my mother found us too much to cope with and decided to send us to St. Mary's, Wantage. One of my maiden aunts was a sister of that community. My mother belonged to a big family; there were eight girls and two boys and she was the only girl who married. My mother's father, a parson, died at fifty-two leaving his widow more or less penniless with eight surviving children. So they all went and lived with her mother, my great-grandmother, in Wren House, a Grace and Favour house at Kensington Palace given her in 1870 in recognition of her services as "the faithful and most devoted nurse of Her Majesty's children, who were much attached to her." When Mrs. Thurston was chosen for her position as head nurse, she was a widow with one little girl (my mother's mother), and this child, Libbie, was brought up with Queen Victoria's children. My early years were very much dominated by Royalty—the model behaviour of the princes and princesses in eating up their pudding and so on.

During her sixteen years' residence at Wren House, Mrs. Thurston was visited by many of the crowned heads of Europe, including the Czar of Russia. At one time she looked after the Kaiser when he was a child in the Isle of Wight. There were lockets in a glass case in my Aunt's drawing-room containing his hair and these used to intrigue us very much as children. The Queen herself used to visit my great-grandmother at Wren House. A special step was built to enable her to get down from her carriage since she was such a small woman. I saw this still in place the other day. I can remember visits from royalty when I was a little girl and being told to behave well and curtsey to the

14

two ladies. But I stared at them rather rudely, so that one of them—I think it was Princess Beatrice—asked me, "Why are you staring, child?" I said, "I'm so disappointed you're not wearing a crown." This is a classic old story, but in my case it actually happened. The Princess was wearing a toque.

I can remember very vividly one visit to Wren House with my nanny and having a hip bath with the fascinating shadows playing from the candlelight and the fire blazing. I must have been only five or six at the time. The *Titanic* disaster made a great impression on my sister and me, and at Kensington Palace—it would be in 1912 —we played going to sea in an old-fashioned linen basket, toppling it over and falling out and singing "Nearer my God to Thee."

My great-grandmother died in 1896 at the age of eighty-five but Queen Victoria allowed my maiden aunts to go on living at Kensington Palace until I was about seventeen. By then my eldest aunt had died, and the others—the nun, the brilliant nurse who ultimately became matron of Northampton General Hospital, and Aunt Elsie, who was secretary to Lord Jersey—were not there very much. Wren House had been in the family for fifty years, which was extremely generous, and now Queen Mary needed it for someone else. It was sad for my aunts having to leave it. My mother had been married from there and the house had so many associations for them.

Through my Aunt Ella, one of the many granddaughters of Mrs. Thurston, my sister and I got reduced fees at Wantage. It was agony saying goodbye to my mother and my home, and my early years at St. Gabriel's House, the junior school, were extremely unhappy. My sister and I were put to share a very small room together, the discipline was very strict, and the religious ritual, which I came to like later on, was rather a shock at first. The nun in charge of us was often unkind and we were very frightened of her. I will say that when I mentioned this to the Mother Superior some years later, she said, "Yes, I'm very sorry. We found out that this woman was not suitable for the younger children." One of this nun's favourite habits was to ask, "Why were you talking in the dormitory last night? I am sure you were discussing things you shouldn't." And usually we had been discussing the facts of life (which now, of course, everybody knows and is most scientific about, but in those days one was left in ignorance), and she told us we were very wicked and disgusting.

The architecture of St. Gabriel's was hideous; even now it makes me shudder. There was a permanent slight smell of gas. I can remember my desperation. Although it was summertime, I was frightened of sleeping in the dark. I think this was because, after the tragedy with my father, my mother had me to sleep in her room and she always had a night-light. Later she let us have one in our bedrooms as children, and at school, of course, this was not allowed. In the dark with the curtains drawn I felt I was going to suffocate. I just had to get over this terror, and I did. But it was a very tough school then. The food was horrible; perhaps in those war years (it was in 1916 that we went to St. Mary's) it was difficult for them to do any better. To have a fresh egg was a very great occasion, but we all, the whole school, had one on Easter morning. The Sister Superior used to come in to have breakfast with us that day. As she entered the room, she said, "Christ is risen" and we answered, "Allelua", but our minds were all on those lovely eggs.

My sister and I were teased unmercifully. I remember being in Coventry for days because the girls said Kathleen curled her hair—it was very pretty and naturally wavy—and I persisted in saying she didn't. Altogether we were subject to great teasing and though we may have deserved it, I can't believe it was good for us to be so unhappy. I would never send a very young child of mine away to school. The uniform was a gym tunic, rather like the shift dress of today, but with this we wore blouses and black stockings, all very unattractive. I don't remember any pleasure in my first year there at all. Our letters home were read before they could be sent off, there was no vestige of personal freedom and the whole approach was really quite Victorian.

The school was at most only thirty miles from home, but we had no cars in those days and my mother used to come and see us only once a year. Then we went out and ate a great many strawberries and cream and other delectable things. After a year I moved to the senior school (at least I was quite well advanced in lessons, as I think children taught by governesses often are) and things began to get better. I started to like the religious part, with Easter the great occasion always. During Lent we had great fun growing flowers for the Easter Cross and collecting rocks, moss and plants to decorate it. All Good Friday until tea-time we kept silence and looked forward very much to breaking it over our hot cross buns. By Easter Saturday the Cross was ready and we had a procession to it when we came out of Chapel after Solemn Evensong, which was always rather wonderful. Some old girls of the school used to come down to spend the weekend, which all added to our excitement.

One of my special treats at the senior school was being allowed to go up on Sundays to the Convent, which stood on a hill and had a beautiful garden. Here I used to walk with my aunt, Sister Marie Fidelia. I remember her telling me the Mother Superior used to read Shakespeare to the other nuns and that this was something they enjoyed very much. Sometimes as we strolled we would suddenly meet the Mother Superior herself; we sank to our knees and she passed on.

I was the youngest girl in my class when I joined the seniors, but there I made a lifelong friend. A girl sitting near me when I arrived gave me a lovely smile. She had beautiful eyes. Her name was Enid Branston, now Tregoning, and to this day she is still beautiful and has the same lovely smile. After the services I'd sat through in our village church, all dressed up and with my hair curled, I found the services in the school chapel, conducted by a very nice chaplain, surprisingly enjoyable. I was confirmed when I was eleven, which was considered very young. I am afraid one of the attractions for me was to get the red book they gave candidates—"Before the Throne". The Sister Superior always kissed you and gave you violets, and you had breakfast with her after your first communion.

Seven of us were being confirmed and for each of us there was a picture one of the nuns had painted, representing the Seven Gifts of the Holy Spirit. As the youngest candidate I was allowed first choice. The pictures were all of angels with wonderful coloured wings. I was very tempted by the red one which was the gift of Wisdom, but in the end felt compelled to choose the gift of Understanding, the angel with pale yellow wings. I am still very conscious of the supreme value of understanding, a form of silent communication which underlies all that I have tried for in life. All healing, undoubtedly, is a bridge or an interpretation or communication, and where understanding and natural sympathy between doctor and patient is weak or non-existent, there is a correspondingly small chance of cure.

My sister, who was also being prepared for confirmation,

showed a great deal of spirit and refused to go to confession. A vital issue was made of this and in the end she wasn't confirmed with me. The whole thing affected her for many years. She was so unhappy that it was finally decided to remove her to another school. There Kathleen settled down much better and later, really, she became more religious than I was throughout her life and was very faithful to the Wantage traditions. She was much cleverer than I, exceptionally good at literature and mathematics —a very gifted person. I was better at using my hands, drawing, sewing and practical things.

When I was just coming up to twelve years old, I won the Royal Drawing Society's silver medal with a drawing of some of the smaller children at school. During a big 'flu epidemic I'd been put in charge of them and this was something which delighted me, for I had always longed to be a governess, maybe because I had a desire to boss people or maybe because I'd been bossed so much myself by governesses. Anyway, I settled these little ones down to do some writing and then I drew them. The drawing was reproduced on the cover of the Royal Drawing Society's magazine, and I remember Sister Catherine saying to me, "Well, Sheila, you're famous now." A picture also appeared in a newspaper with the caption "Child Genius". Mother was very proud. I still have the drawing today and when occasionally I exhibit it, it is still always noticed.

I was very bad at arithmetic. It was not until I came into business that I began to get an interest in figures; they seemed then to mean something to me. Geometry and Algebra, yes, I could do them because they were visual. Towards the end of my time at school, the Head Sister said, "You could get to Oxford. Would you like to have a go?" I was horrified, for all my maiden aunts had told me that men did not like clever women. I thought it would be dreadful to be a bluestocking. So I said, "Oh no, I don't want to do that," and she was quite disappointed.

It was then decided that I must go to school in Paris, and this time my grandfather paid the fees for mother. We were always in money troubles. My mother had so little and had never been trained to manage on her own. Then there was this terrible business of keeping up with the Joneses. Although one has it today, I don't think it's anything like so bad as it was then. We were living in a very small house in the country, surrounded by enormous mansions and very grand people, and we couldn't possibly compete in this world. At one time my mother wanted to take a house in Cheltenham and send us to Cheltenham College, but our grandfather had insisted it must be Wantage. Certainly I was very sad when I left there because my last year had been a very happy one. This was partly because I took the domestic science course. We did this three days a week and I believe I've still got my certificate from the London School of Domestic Arts. I passed, I think, with 93% or something like that. The requirements included making the purchases for a meal and cooking it, doing laundry (all very primitive in those days, no mod. cons.) and cleaning out rooms really thoroughly—a major operation we were well drilled in, and I did enjoy it. My great friend Enid, the pretty one, was with me on this course and we worked together. On cookery days we ate the meals we cooked, which was a great attraction. Even then I had a hatred of meat, and another friend of mine, Valerie Dyas, who relished it, used to cut mine up for me because it made me feel sick to touch it and look at it. So the seeds of vegetarianism were already there, and in fact at Wantage a lot of my meat went to feed the dog. I used to drop it into my handkerchief and take it to him.

The day came when we left. We all cried and were very miserable. In spite of my criticism of Wantage during my early days there, I am very grateful for what they did for me. They certainly gave me a discipline for life, but I think I was sent much too young. I don't think children should leave home until they are at least thirteen or fourteen. It was summertime and there was the excitement of going to Paris. A friend of my mother, Mrs. Cadogan, who lived at Hatherop Castle (now Miss Fyfe's School) had recommended the establishment of Mademoiselle Duvernet, and three other new pupils and myself were met in London to be escorted there. I made a new friend I've kept for life, Ann Bovill. At the age of thirty she became Woman's Editor of the *Daily Mirror* and she was a brilliant girl. I remember that I'd put up my hair while hers was still down her back, and she was very annoyed mine was up and hers down. I fancy we were both about seventeen then. The two other girls were daughters of rich industrialists from the north. They had enormous wardrobes of clothes and a vast amount of money. Both of them cried solidly for the first week. Mademoiselle Duvernet wouldn't let my friend and me share a bedroom but made each of us take one of the rich girls. We used to envy them madly because they went to the Opera every week while we went only once a month. They couldn't speak a word of French so we had separate classes, and I had a professor to teach me fashion drawing. He was quite unsuitable, grey-bearded M. Jean Bremond, but anyway I used to do drawings for him which were entirely original. I have some of them still and find them intriguing to look through. Lacking the dress allowances of some of my contemporaries, I had made my own clothes for a long time—even a bridesmaid's dress for a very grand wedding at St. Margaret's, Westminster. The other bridesmaids went to Revelle to have their dresses made; mine was cut out for me and I made it myself. It looked just as good as theirs, but I remember feeling terribly self-conscious. Nowadays, of course, I should be proud of having made it. It seems extraordinary to me now, this attitude of not wanting people to know I'd done it myself, but I was so overpowered by the wealth of others and the splendid way they lived. At the dressmaking classes in Paris I was so ahead of the rest that I used to spend my time helping them cut things out and make them up. I enjoyed this, but there were other much more exciting pastimes.

On certain days of the week we used to go sight-seeing in Paris. I was absolutely thrilled with the Louvre and all the palaces, we visited museums, and we used to go quite a lot to Versailles and walk in the gardens there. This was a tremendous treat for me. I thought the visits to the Opera something out of this world. We used to dress up in full evening dress and go in the tube. There was great excitement, Frenchmen pressing up against us and so on, and more of them to look at in the interval of the Opera when we walked round to see and be seen. All the schoolgirls there used to sit in boxes; my friend and I loved it and longed to be able to go more often.

We also went shopping and I made myself a fantastic green taffeta dress which I wore at hunt balls later when I went home in the holidays. Obviously I had a gift and I was offered a job as a designer in a Paris shop, but my mother said I must come out in London, and I did go to some balls, even though I couldn't really afford to do the season properly. It seems to me now that I fell between two stools having rich relations and so little money. My paternal grandfather had come to live in an enormous mansion in what is now known as Millionaires' Row: 12a, Kensington Palace Gardens. (It's the Nepalese Embassy today. The Russian Embassy is next door and I can remember their arrival there.) All was incredibly luxurious. There was a staff of eighteen, a very grand butler and two footmen. I used to enjoy the vast rooms and the generally big sort of life, very different from the genteel poverty of my maiden aunts on the other side of the field in Wren House. They with their royal connections were inclined to regard the richer side of the family as rather parvenu. Even while I enjoyed staying at my grandfather's, I was always a bit overcome, shadowed by the feeling of being a poor relation. And my mother was very nervous going there, which I can now understand very well. London itself had always a magic for me, from childhood visits when I was taken to Barkers to see Father Christmas, and Kensington Gardens where the old lady sold balloons. The Underground was terribly exciting to me then. Going down in the lift the notice "Mind your handbags" made us grip ours. Coming from the country, we felt we were having a big adventure. Then down in the Tube were the roaring trains and the marvellous posters on the walls—this was really seeing life. I remember particularly the poster of a play called *Romance*, starring Doris Keene; she wore a beautiful black dress. That we weren't allowed to go to this play, which was considered unsuitable for us, only added to the attraction.

Despite our lack of money, the idea of my earning my own living seemed quite wrong to my mother. When I was seventeen, a friend offered to finance me in a dress shop but my mother refused this, just as she did the opening for me as a designer in Paris. If I have a regret in life, I regret that I didn't have a proper métier, as the French say. I could have been a successful dress designer, I am certain of that. I could also have been a good portrait painter. But I was devoted to my mother and it never entered my head to leave her and strike out on my own; it was not till I was older that I did this.

When I went home simply thrilled with this autumn term in Paris, to my great joy I was told I could stay another term. I think that again my grandfather paid for me, which was kind of him. My friend Ann and I came back by train and boat and train, as one did in those days. We had each made ourselves a new hat and were very dolled up to meet our mothers at Victoria station.

But the passage was frightfully rough and we suddenly felt sick. We went below and had to share a bunk. It was so crowded and quite awful, the seasickness and discomfort. And I lay on my hat and we were both very bedraggled when we got to London.

At dances that winter at home I was considered very extreme because I had a long dress when people were wearing them shorter. I can remember the terrible worry of getting partners in those days. Having no father or brothers we seemed to know no men at all. At this time, owing to the shortage of men, the invitations came for "Miss Craven and partner". My sister and I found it extremely difficult to find anyone and were terrified of being wallflowers. I envied those with a comfortable background of having men around naturally. Until I was twenty-one I was never allowed out alone with a man but always chaperoned.

After Christmas I went back to Paris. One excitement I remember vividly. We always went to the English church in the Rue Auguste Vacquerie. A governess went with us and used to go to her own church. On one occasion when we came out to meet her in a café—we had breakfast after Mass—she wasn't there. She'd had a very long service and then forgot all about us. So my friend and I went round Paris on our own, feeling frightful devils. We went up the Arc de Triomphe and finally got back to school quite all right, but Mademoiselle Duvernet was almost fainting with agitation and the poor governess was in terrible trouble.

2

AT THE END of my time in Paris I had a great excitement and also a great worry. My mother and sister had gone to Bordighera in Italy, on a shoestring as usual, and Kathleen was taken most terribly ill. They were supposed to be meeting me in Paris but this was impossible, so I went to the South of France where my grandfather was staying with his wife and two daughters. They were living in great luxury at Cannes, with a whole suite at the top of a big hotel, for they travelled with chauffeurs and servants as people did in those days. And I went down on a night train, a great thrill. Mademoiselle put me in a compartment, and when I arrived my grandfather said, "Why on earth didn't you come in a sleeper! A young girl like yourself shouldn't travel alone at night." I replied that I didn't think we could afford it, but all the same I felt glad he had a thought for my welfare.

It was wonderful in the South of France. I responded to the beauty of it all and felt very lucky. We played tennis a good deal, but there didn't seem to be many young people. I was very strictly chaperoned and never allowed out without a maid to go with me, even when I went to church. After we returned to England, my sister arrived, still dreadfully ill—I shall never forget meeting her—and we went back to our house in the country. I felt very flat. I had nothing to do really except play tennis, do the flowers and make clothes for other people, who used to pay me thirty shillings for a dress, a pound for a blouse. About this time my great friend Margaret Evetts became engaged to be married and she asked me to make her dress, her veil and several other things for her trousseau. This gave me immense pleasure and I dressed the bride on the morning of her wedding. I also made myself a coat and dress to wear for this occasion, but I had my first disaster with the coat. I had used synthetic lining, put too hot an iron on it and the whole piece came away with the iron. There was no time to repair it, as I was pressing the coat just before the wedding, so I had to keep my coat shut most of the time! It was at Margaret's wedding that I met Douglas Blew Jones, who introduced me to Francis ten years later.

My sister also became engaged to be married and I was a bridesmaid at her wedding. At the reception there was a friend of Ulick Brown the dress designer, and she sent me along to see him because she thought I would be suitable as a model girl. I had an interview with him and he gave me some lovely dresses to put on, walk about in and show him whether I was able to do it. I was very thrilled at the end when he offered me a permanent job; I thought that now I was really getting somewhere, but my mother said, "Oh no, you are far too young to go and live by yourself. You can't possibly do that." So back I went to the country.

By now my first love affair had been well and truly broken off. I'd been jilted by a glamorous young man I had met in the South of France at a ball. I thought I'd never met anyone so wonderful and so handsome—I was thrilled he'd asked to be introduced to me. He had brown and white shoes and a car and a chauffeur, which seemed to me the last word in elegance. Though I didn't know it at the time, my admirer had just had an upset with his girl friend. Probably this had something to do with his asking me to marry him. At any rate when I got back to England he met me at the station and said he'd changed his mind. I was very upset and never wiped out the memory of him until three years later in the Canary Islands. There I unfortunately fell in love with a married man old enough to be my father. And this is enough about my early romances (if they can be called so) except to say that I think some providence has always watched over me and I've been taught lessons without going through the hard experience I might have done. I have had some extremely lucky escapes in my life.

I was very unsettled when, through an aunt with whom I was staying, I had an offer of a job I was allowed to accept. That autumn I presented myself at the dress shop *Marguerite* at number 9, Old Bond Street, where I was to work for Madge Hayward, my aunt's friend, the owner of it. Rather ungratefully, I hated it. Having lived free in the country and got used to fresh air, I felt I couldn't stand the heat and being penned up all day. But nothing would have induced me to admit to my mother that I didn't like it. She had been so worried about my coming to London that she came up herself and took a little flat in the Fulham Road. I was twenty-one at the time and my current admirer brought me up in his car with my mother and all our bits and pieces. He used to come and take me out, and after a few months he proposed to me. Apart from becoming engaged to marry him—which was called off later—I began to have rather an exciting time at the dress shop. We started having dress shows and I was terrified my grandfather would find out, because he strongly disapproved of the whole thing and thought I was making myself cheap.

Then came a holiday in the Canary Islands with my mother, which would have been wonderful if I hadn't fallen violently in love with this married man. My poor mother was dreadfully upset. I realise now that I was looking for a father substitute, but anyway it all ended in fiasco and when I came back to England I decided to go back to my old job. Then began a very wild and gay time. We were much fêted, as all model girls are, we had terrific lunches out and a trail of boy-friends and admirers. When I went home in the summer holidays, my mother was very ill. She picked up chicken-pox, and I nursed her. Then my sister caught it, and I nursed her. When our local doctor pronounced me out of quarantine I went back to the dress shop. But as I was changing one day, I saw a spot on my leg. "Heavens!" I said to my employer, "I've got chicken-pox." "You can't have. How do you know?" she asked in the greatest consternation. I explained how my sister had had it but that I had been cleared. "Go home," she said, "go away." There was a wedding coming off quite soon, I'd kissed the bride, and altogether I felt absolutely terrible about all this. The small private hotel in Cromwell Road where I was living at the time wouldn't keep me, no-one would come near me, and by then I was getting covered in spots. I hired a car at huge expense and arrived home only to be told I couldn't stay there. My mother had let the house and was going away.

So I had to lodge in a cottage in the village with a policeman's widow, who was none too willing and said that if I gave her chicken-pox I'd have to stay to look after her. She had the habit of coming into my bedroom and saying in a gruesome voice, "This is the bed my husband died in." It was all rather a ghastly experience for a young person and really I'd have done better to go to the fever hospital in London. I think I got up too soon, I was so bored and miserable, and I used to walk all over the countryside when I certainly wasn't fit for it. This must have had a bad effect on my nerves because later that autumn I had a breakdown. It was to take me the best part of two years to get over that. I was finally restored to health by meeting a wonderful healer. She did not use drugs and she herself had had a miraculous recovery from Bright's Disease. She used to talk to me and give me absent healing, and it was entirely through her that I was able to lead a completely normal life again. I learnt a great deal from her about prayer and meditation and constructive thoughts.

During this time my mother, who had had arthritic troubles, got progressively worse, and this had a deep and lasting effect on me. She suffered so much pain and was so terribly unhappy. I am quite certain that my father's death and the scandal and secrecy of it had all affected her and that she was suffering from what in these modern times would be called stress, bringing on this dreadful illness. When she was recovering a little and I was over my breakdown, we had the idea of going to stay in France. In fact, we'd taken a villa there and were getting ready to travel when Britain went off the gold standard, which made things difficult. I don't know what gave me the idea—somewhere I must have heard about the attractions of Estoril in Portugal—but anyway I said, "Let's go there." My mother demurred a bit, saying they were always having revolutions, but I said I didn't think that mattered much, so off we went. We took with us a wonderful maid companion, Hester Norris, who'd come to look after mother when she was so ill, and a girl friend of mine, Eve Hall, joined us too.

We immediately fell in love with Estoril. Portugal was a marvellous country, and still is from what I hear from friends, and in fact I've been back twice myself since that visit. I'm afraid we were absolute idlers, my friend and I. We played golf— there was a delightful nine-hole course, now it's an eighteen-hole one—and one morning, to my intense excitement, I did a hole in one. To this day I have the certificate confirming it. It was a short hole, I drove off and when we got to the green we couldn't find my ball. Naturally we were thrilled when one of the caddies finally looked in the hole and there it was. We used to dance most of the night and swim on the beaches, where we also had splendid picnics, with the whole of the sands to ourselves. It was quite incredible. Needless to say, I fell violently in love with an unsuitable man once more. He was married and extremely charming. Everybody has gay love affairs in Portugal and you wake up laughing. It's the only country I can think of where one really does that all the time, or one did in those days.

We spent the whole winter there and it was an exceptionally fine one, I've been told. What is more, we lived for under three pounds a week, with a sitting room and bedrooms. Very good food and a spacious life. It was still quite feudal—people had troops of servants—and there was terrible poverty, though even so everyone seemed smiling and happy. Society there was rather dominated by the German Ambassador, Freddie Horstmann, who lived like a prince of the eighteenth century in a most beautiful palace. He gave wonderful parties and had famous musicians to play for him. His chef had been with the King of the Belgians and he had a number of footmen who impressed me with their magnificence. Sometimes he gave very amusing parties on the beach and there were also informal dances where we used to do the tango in the moonlight.

Later this man had a most terrible time. When the Russians occupied East Germany he was living on his estate, though the Manor House had been destroyed by allied bombs. He had collected round him a few of his beautiful possessions, for he was a great connoisseur of the arts, and he refused to leave, saying that he must look after them. Then one night he was taken and he died of starvation in a concentration camp near his home. I was told he held his courage to the last.

It was sad when our Portuguese holiday had to come to an end. My mother's health hadn't improved and we thought it would be better to return to England. We took a house in Mayfield in Sussex, but all the time my mother was getting worse and worse. She was forever trying different treatments and injections and terrible things were done to her. At Christmas 1932 she said to me, "If this doesn't do me good . . ." (some new drug or other) "I just don't feel I can try to go on living." Finally she got so bad that she had to go to a nursing home down in Torquay. I took a small room in London and led a sort of bed-sitter life in South Kensington, with frequent visits to Torquay, never quite knowing what was going to happen or when I would be wanted. I used to stay in a small hotel near the nursing home.

She died in Torquay that June. I used to implore the doctors to leave her alone, stop all these drugs and injections, but they would not. This was what implanted in me a deep distrust of doctors and orthodox methods, for I saw how devastating they could be. My mother became mentally ill at the end. It was dreadful to see her as she was then. She had four nurses to look after her and used to ask me to take her out for a drive as I'd once been in the habit of doing; now we had to pretend we went while I sat at her bedside. Later she thought I had taken all her money. It was the other way round actually; I was living on a shoestring in this one room in London and naturally the nursing home was very expensive. Despite this long illness, my mother's death was a terrible shock to me. I suppose I had never faced up to life properly before, and as for death, we had always been kept away from anything to do with it. It sounds stupid to have been so ignorant at the age of twenty-seven, but seeing her coffin lowered into the earth was an experience I shall never forget. I was devoted to her, it had been so harrowing to see her crippled and ill, and now to die in this dreadful way. There was no-one to stand with me at the graveside. My sister Kathleen was in India with her husband, and I had, of course, neither father nor brothers nor any close relation to come. I knew real loneliness then. One thinks of these things happening to other people's mothers, not one's own. It took me time to take this in and begin to stand on my own feet, as I've had to do throughout the rest of my life.

I went down to Eastbourne to recover a little and stayed in a strange house with a lady who was very psychic. She told me I had the aura of a healer. I also made friends with an actor who was staying there, and I remember him telling me, "You won't be much good or come into your own until you're about forty." And I thought, "That's rather a long time," but was quite intrigued.

At first my grandfather told me that there was nothing to come to Kathleen and myself from my mother. I felt a bit shaken; however, I knew I had earned my living before, and now mother was dead and I could do no more for her, I felt I could earn it again. As it turned out, my grandfather was mistaken, for though he had wanted to cut us out of his will, he had made settlements he must have forgotten about. A cousin of mine, Sir Charles Craven, a man in big business whom I got to know quite well, rang me up and said, "You're all right, you've been left a few hundreds a year, you and your sister." This was only one occasion on which this cousin was extremely kind to me.

My grandfather asked me to come and see him. He was in the library of his enormous house in Kensington Palace Gardens, with the family lawyer, Mr. Ryan, who had come up from Manchester. Mr. Ryan said to me, "You may never marry; you had better take out an insurance." I suddenly saw red. "Probably I shan't," I said. "What I want to do is to travel. I am going to India and I don't care if I have to borrow the money, I am going." They both looked a bit shaken but that was that. I began to make arrangements to go out and stay with my sister.

3

I BOOKED myself a passage on a boat called *Strathaird* and off
I set for India. It was a marvellous voyage. I travelled with a
very nice girl, Rosemary Stanley, whose uncle was Governor
of Madras, so when we arrived we were met by a most magnificent A.D.C. The friend who was to meet me never turned up,
so Rosemary and the A.D.C. looked after me and I had my first
glimpse of Imperial India which was, of course, very grand
indeed. They found my train in the end and I got on to it. I was
going to stay with a friend whose husband had to do with the
railways; I'd always wondered why she hated it, but I soon saw
that the social grading in India was so terrible that if you weren't
in the right set and happened to be a sensitive woman, it must be
very trying. Another thing I found was that the men all thought
I'd come in search of a husband. This was an extraordinary
attitude to my way of thinking. All the same, I did love seeing
that part of India. We went to Udaipur, which is a most beautiful
city, surrounded by water; they call it, I believe, the Venice of
India. I was taken to see an elephant stable in the Palace. They
had elephants of all ages and a lot of baby ones which were very
charming. These elephants are used a great deal in ceremonial
processions as well as for other purposes. They keep them just
as we have a stable of horses here. We also went to Bundi, the
rose-red city, where I met the Maharaja's wife in purdah. She
thought it strange that I was travelling by myself. The Maharaja's
son, a young boy of about seven, interpreted for us because the
Maharanee didn't speak English.

Next I travelled by train up to the frontier, to Peshawar, and
stayed with my sister among the Indian Army. I really wasn't
very happy there, though it wasn't anybody's fault except my
own: I just didn't seem to fit in. I liked being with the political
people and having a chance to go and meet Indians. I also had
some very nice riding while I was there. I hadn't ridden for a
great many years and went out in a riding school which was

rather terrifying. There was a Sergeant Major on a prancing horse; we all had to ride round him and gallop, and I thought to myself I'd be lucky if I didn't fall off. My horse had a very hard mouth. However, after this episode one of the officers very kindly lent me a rather quiet horse and I had some nice peaceful rides with him. I was glad I did this because when I got to Abyssinia not long after this I really had to take up riding seriously and I should have felt a fool if I hadn't been able to do it.

On the *Strathaird* I made friends with a man who knew Lady Willingdon, the Vicereine at that time. He mentioned me to her and to my great amazement there came a letter inviting me to stay at the Viceroy's House. This threw everybody in this military stronghold into an absolute flutter and I realised I was extremely lucky to have such an invitation. Some of the women painted a rather frightening picture of Lady Willingdon. Her efficiency was a legend and of course the position she held was very magnificent. So I packed up and left wondering what lay ahead. It was certainly an adventure for me.

I had an Indian servant, a rather strange little man who'd been engaged for me while I was staying at Ajmer, and he went with me on this journey to Delhi. We travelled by train and when we came to a stop after the first day, the Stationmaster came with a sort of policewoman who said, "Don't unlock your door through the night, whatever you do. There's been trouble on the trains and you must be careful." This did rather give me the creeps. You didn't have corridors on the trains in those days, and you heard all these milling people trying to climb in, looking for a lift. Some soldiers in another compartment said, "Why don't you come in with us?" I answered that I didn't think it would look very suitable if I arrived to stay with the Viceroy sleeping with a whole lot of officers. "Perhaps you're right," they said, "but at every station we'll get out and tap on the window." They were very kind to me. All the same, I had a bad night and overslept, which was terrible because I wasn't ready when I arrived in Delhi, and a magnificent gentleman, covered in cocks' feathers and swords and cords and goodness knows what, was waiting for me. Somehow they got me out of the train and into the car.

We drove up the most tremendous avenue to the Viceroy's house, and I remember a famous cartoon drawn by Bateman of a very tiny little man going to Buckingham Palace; I must say I

31

felt rather like this. The House was most impressive. There were mounted guards who belonged to a crack Indian regiment, wonderful-looking men, and an enormous household staff of Indians. A very friendly English butler met me and took me up to a lovely room looking out on a dream garden, one of Lady Willingdon's special interests.

I went to a Ball which was a splendidly formal occasion. At lunch that same day I met His Excellency for the first time. Afterwards the A.D.C. came up to me and said, "You're going to have Number Five with His Excellency tonight." I was very thrilled and my cup was full. Lady Willingdon was tremendously kind to me, especially over the loss of my mother, and told me I was wise to travel. When she knew I was determined to see the Taj Mahal she told me, "Either you must go with your best boy-friend or on your own." She made arrangements for me to be met and looked after at the station when I arrived at Agra. As I hadn't a boy-friend, I took her advice and went on my own, getting up in the dawn. The Taj Mahal is a truly magnificent sight. The moon was just waning and the beauty of it all is something I shall always remember.

When I left Agra I travelled to Calcutta where I stayed a few days. David MacEwen was there; I had met him briefly in England and we had travelled out together. It was very nice to see him again, and he has been a friend of mine ever since. Rosemary Stanley, whom I'd met on the *Strathaird*, invited me to Madras to stay with her uncle, Sir George Stanley, who was Governor there. So once again I visited a beautiful house, surrounded by servants and charming A.D.C.s, and we enjoyed ourselves immensely. While I was there I learnt to surf. We used to go to a beach about five miles away from Government House. There were some marvellous rollers. I got on these surf boards and managed to get the knack of it—I was a bit scared but didn't want the A.D.C.s to know this—and it is a wonderful feeling skimming in on the surf. Altogether it was a very happy time there and I was so grateful to the Stanleys for having me to stay.

Another introduction I was given when I left led to an invitation to visit Government House, Bombay. There again we used to go out to a splendid beach and have some marvellous bathing. I was also taken out sailing in a small yacht, which I found delightful.

I thought India was a most wonderful country. The people are

Sheila, aged 4.

Mother, Sheila and Kathleen.

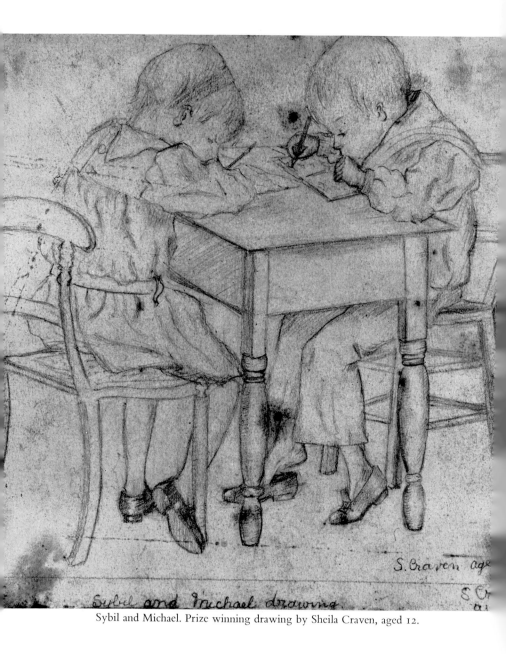

Sybil and Michael. Prize winning drawing by Sheila Craven, aged 12.

intensely spiritual and you could feel this everywhere. They must be hundreds of years ahead of the Western world in spiritual matters. We are now ahead of them in material things, but I think their influence is spreading to the West. The fact that in this day and age they have a woman as Prime Minister is very significant. Only thirty years ago, when I was there, Lady Willingdon told me that she had five hundred cases of women who were still in purdah and who wished to escape from it, and that she was trying to help them.

The other thing which struck me immediately was the wonderful light there, the quick change from day to night with very little twilight, and there was something very mysterious about this sudden nightfall. I loved this quiet moment when day slipped so quickly into night.

On the voyage out to India, I met a girl called Esme Barton who played a great part in my life. She was on her way to Abyssinia and said I must go and stay with them there, just to send her a cable from India to say when. Now I thought, "Well, why not?" so I got on a boat which would take me as far as Aden. "You'll be met and stay with the Resident," Esme had said. By this time I'd got very grand and used to the red carpet—I'm afraid one gets into this way, it's all too easy. When I arrived in Aden I was met and taken to a very dusty hotel and I didn't like this at all. "Why am I not staying at the Residency?" I said. "Oh well, I don't know," said the A.D.C. "Bernard Reilly's not expecting you. Yes, he did get a telegram, but his name was spelt wrong, which infuriates him, and besides he's a bachelor and I suppose he doesn't want women guests." "Oh dear!" I said. But the man who'd met me turned out quite sporting and suggested we should go to the Club for a drink and see what happened when the Resident came in. He took one look at me and said, "No-one told me you were coming. I thought it was some cricketer. Fetch Miss Craven's bags at once," he ordered. So that came off all right.

We made great friends before I set off on my next lap of the journey, and a very extraordinary one this was. In those days you went by sea from Aden to Djibouti, and it was very, very hot. I had a small cabin below, and when I looked down it was just a seething mass of cockroaches. "I can't sleep here," I thought, and carted my sleeping things—at that time we travelled with immense paraphernalia—up on deck. Everybody got drunk, including the Captain. The mate came over and told me he'd had D.T.s, and it was a terrifying experience really. There was a Somali on the helm. Fortunately it was a very calm night and eventually we reached Djibouti. In the morning the old skipper said to me, "A nice young lady like you oughtn't to be travelling round the world by yourself," and he gave me a set of charms which he said would bring me a husband. Strangely enough I've kept these charms. Francis always takes one on his Atlantic voyages, and various other ones I've lent to friends.

From Djibouti it took three days and two nights to get up to Addis Ababa at its eight thousand two hundred feet. There I was met by Esme and had a wonderfully happy time with the Bartons. They were extremely kind to me and gave me a family life which I had never really known before. I shall never forget it, and in fact that was why later on I asked Sir Sidney to give me away at my wedding, I had become so attached to him and to Lady Barton. There were only three girls in this diplomatic community and about fifty men to choose from. We used to ride everywhere because of the altitude, and in the evening we would dance. I shall always remember galloping across the plains and the wind whistling through my pony's ears. A very charming Belgian officer who, with two or three others, was training the Abyssinian Army, used to lend me this pony called Gonda. It had a beautifully light mouth; the officer never allowed his grooms to ride these ponies, only to lead them.

I was presented to the Emperor during this visit. Sir Sidney Barton took me, we drove in state and I saw what they called the Dance of the Priests, which was the same dance, I believe, as David did before the Ark of the Lord. It was all very impressive and very interesting. But the Italians were then plotting and planning to take Abyssinia; Sir Sidney knew that and was very disapproving of anybody Italian.

Well, all good things come to an end. With a terrible feeling of flatness I started on my journey back to England. On the way, I stayed in Aden with Sir Bernard Reilly, and the same ship, the *Strathaird*, picked me up. Some friends from India were aboard and I had a great welcome. I found Sir Eric Mieville there; he was private secretary to Lord Willingdon and later was to become secretary to the Duke of York, the future George VI. There were also Sir Alexander Hore-Ruthven and his wife, on their way from Australia, where he was later Governor-General. We left the ship at Port Sudan and motored through the desert to Cairo. Sir Miles Lampson, the High Commissioner, took me to see some tombs near the Pyramids which had just been opened. I was told to look through a little peephole at a tiny effigy put there to guard the soul of the departed. "You are one of the first people to see that," a professor told me. It must have been thousands of years old. We also visited another ceremonial tomb they had uncovered, made in the shape of a boat because the Egyptians believed this was how the soul travelled on its journey to the next life. I found all this fascinating. Sir Miles Lampson was a wonderful host, and later in the evening we returned by train to the ship which had come through the Canal to Port Said. Here Jack Hulbert and some of his fellow actors joined us. They had been making a film, "A Date in the Desert". Jack Hulbert sat at table with me and he really was a most delightful companion, keeping us all in fits of laughter.

It was a marvellous voyage, making me feel even lonelier when I got back to London, for there was no mother waiting for me now and my sister and her husband were still in India. There I was, all this grand and interesting life behind me, and at a dead end. I decided to find myself a flat and took one in Chelsea, in a new block called Sloane Avenue Mansions, where I stayed until I married. It was a very, very modern place and we had every kind of convenience, a garage, a restaurant, maid and valet service. I passed a very solitary winter. I took up bridge but found it terrifying when I got among good players. Not that I was a bad player myself, but they did it for money and for a living, and if you made one mistake, they'd say you had cost them a hat or something. It wasn't my going at all.

Having decided I couldn't bear the bridge, I made up my mind to go back to Portugal where I'd been so happy. I stayed with a friend in a rather nice hotel and we had a certain amount of fun, but it wasn't quite the same and began to pall after a while. Back in England I went to stay with friends in Devon. They lived at Westward Ho and I had some very happy times there, for I really do love the country, and by then I had taken up golf more seriously. There is a very good course overlooking the sea. Then I had another trip to France, Spain and Portugal. I motored round and that was very interesting. It was just before the Spanish

War, and at one frontier they tried to search me. Luckily I managed to explain I was an English tourist and got away with it, but wherever you went you had either the raised fist or the Fascist salute. One had the roads to oneself, but they were very bad. On one occasion we had to jack the car up out of a rut, very different from modern conditions. My son laughs now when I say, "Oh how wonderful this car is!" but in comparison it's all so easy.

I came back to England still feeling at a loose end. A man friend—a single one this time, who'd wanted me to marry him before I went on these travels—asked me to stay at Bournemouth with him and his mother for Christmas. Christmas was a time I dreaded because I always seemed to be on my own, and then especially I thought of my mother and how I missed her. But for some reason I was cautious, and though I agreed to go, I said I wouldn't stay at their hotel, the Royal Bath, but went to another. And I remember having lunch alone on Christmas Day after all, because by that time I'd made up my mind I couldn't marry him. The manager of my hotel sent me up some flowers saying, "It's terrible that someone like you should be alone at Christmas."

Then I went on to Devon to stay with the Blew Jones at Westward Ho, and that was when I met Francis. We were sitting by the fire when Francis, who'd been out shooting with my host and another friend, walked in holding a dead goose. I was repelled by this because I don't like killing. However, he laughed and I thought he seemed quite nice. I was giving a dinner party that night; I had asked one or two guests and wanted another man, so I said to the other girl in the party, "Shall I ask that man? Would you like him to come?" And she said, "Oh yes, he seems quite nice, let's have him."

The dinner party wasn't a great success. One of the men got terribly sozzled and it was very embarrassing. However, we survived, and the next night, which was New Year's Eve if I remember rightly, we all went to a hunt ball. There was a house-party in Cornwall and Francis came and stayed. I thought what well-cut clothes he had for a man who had come from the Dominions. Later I discovered that his evening clothes had been made by the Duke of Windsor's tailor. In those days one tended to look on people from New Zealand as being a bit uncivilised, but anyway Francis made quite a set at me and I felt his personality. I was going on to a ball in Winchester and had made up my mind I wasn't going to tire myself out motoring, for I'd heard of a service whereby you could put your car on to the train and take it with you. This, of course, is a commonplace now, but at the time it was considered rather original. It amused Francis very much and he went with me to make arrangements.

Next morning I took the train at Bideford. To my amazement Francis jumped into it when we stopped at Instow, and he went straight to the point. He said, "I've got on the train to ask you to marry me." And he added, "I've got an overdraft of fourteen thousand pounds, some trees, a hundred pounds in the bank and that's all." And I remember I was rather startled and said to him, "Well, you know, I spend fifty pounds a year on my hair." "I'd like you to do that," he said. Men are so impractical. Though most people thought me a great deal richer than I was because of my millionaire grandfather, I had in fact just inherited a thousand pounds from an aunt, my father's sister. She had been in the house the night my father committed suicide and had always blamed herself for going off to bed without realising how it was with him. I was very fond of her, and when she died— which was the autumn before I met Francis—I remember thinking, "This is the last older person" (she was only in her fifties) "and now she's gone I'm even more alone." My grandfather too was dead by now, leaving all my cousins very well off. But of course I had no place in his will, whereas my aunt had left me this sum of money for which I was eternally grateful.

But back to Francis's whirlwind proposal. "Well, anyway," I thought, "this is an interesting man." "We're both fairly mature," I said to him, "and we've lived alone. We might be able to make a go of it." He seemed sure I'd enjoy New Zealand, and since my mother had been out there when she first married, I had heard many stories of it, glorified of course. "I'll think about it," I promised. Francis got off the train at Exeter and I thought what a strange experience it had been.

I arrived at Winchester and drove my car off. When I asked a few old friends what they thought about my marrying Francis, they were very disapproving. "You can't do that, he's got no money." This was the male point of view. When I asked Hester, my mother's old maid who had come to look after me at the flat for the winter, "What do you think?" she said, "Well, I think he sounds rather good, quite different from all the others you've had. I always worried about you taking up with these married men." So I said we'd see. When I got back to London, Francis telephoned me and asked how I felt about it. I said I'd write and give him my answer. "I think we might make a success of our lives together," those were my words. It was arranged that he'd come up to London and have dinner at my flat. I'd been given some tickets for a box at the theatre, which was lucky and seemed a good idea. I prepared a nice dinner for Francis, and I think Hester came up to help me, I can't quite remember. Anyhow Francis arrived and he sat down and said, "You know, I've been thinking it over. I don't think I can get married—I'm so used to being alone, and I don't think I'd like to do it." "I absolutely understand how you feel," I said, "but let's go to the theatre all the same. Don't feel tied at all, because it's a dreadful feeling and it would be stupid." So we said no more about it then.

Next morning he turned up again; I don't quite remember what did happen but he told me he'd changed his mind, he did want us to get married. So we became engaged very quickly like that. This was the beginning of January and we were married on February 25, 1937.

4

I DID NOT realise that Francis was a famous aviator until the Press rang me up after our engagement was announced. They told me they had pictures of my fiancé because of his flying achievements, but had none of me. I'd never taken much interest in the air, but now Francis said he would take me up in the plane he'd flown from New Zealand. This was a flight not a great deal written about but a very interesting one, nevertheless. He had got a farmer to stump up the money to buy the plane and they flew home together with Francis as pilot. They'd hoped to go to Russia but hadn't managed this. Anyway, Francis took me down to an aerodrome near London for this trip. In those days I was tremendously dressed up and my outfit was quite unsuitable for going in this plane. It was an open one and I thought I was going to fall out. When one motor stopped, I believed my last hour had come, but I think we were only landing. We glided over a railway line and touched down safely. I must say I was thankful to get my feet on the ground again. This was my first flight and it rather scared me, but I am very glad that I went.

During this time I gave a small party in my flat and invited some of Francis's friends. Amy Johnson came and I well remember her sitting on the sofa beside me and saying to me: "Do you realise you are marrying one of the best navigators in the world? I came to London specially to get him to give me some lessons, and now you're marrying him and going off to New Zealand; I'll have to go to America and find Commander Weems to teach me."

There seemed a great deal to do before our wedding. Francis rushed me along, saying I was to give up my flat and take my furniture to New Zealand and so on, but somehow all this got arranged. I tried to get Hester to go with me but she wouldn't hear of it, though she was very much in favour of the marriage. And I remember Dame Edith Lyttleton saying to me, "I never thought you'd have the sense to marry someone like Francis."

I'm always lucky, and though I complain about the lack of money, this was largely because of the contrast with my very rich relations. At this point I was very grateful indeed for my aunt's legacy, which helped with my trousseau. I got myself some rather good clothes; I always had a great weakness for these. When I first got the money I thought I'd like to buy myself a nice diamond brooch (I was very impractical in those days). But a friend said, "Don't do that; I'm quite certain you won't marry a rich man. Have an aquamarine—you can get one for under a hundred pounds—and then your poor fiancé, if he does come along, won't have to give you a solitaire diamond to match the brooch." So I went to Cartier and did get myself a very beautiful clip brooch with an aquamarine, which I have to this day. When I became engaged to Francis we got a lovely aquamarine ring at what was quite a reasonable figure in those days, and so everybody was happy.

We were married at Chelsea Old Church, later destroyed by a flying bomb but now rebuilt. I wasn't very keen on a church wedding, which may sound strange in view of my religious background, but I think you promise so much in a church and I'd seen so many married people not taking their vows seriously, as I knew I must do if I made them. Francis was the one who was adamant, saying we must have a proper church wedding even though, apart from anything else, I felt I was rather mature for that sort of thing. Finally I agreed, and Sir Sidney Barton, the former ambassador in Addis Ababa, gave me away. The Barton family saw to everything and were extremely good to me. Mollie Craven, my grandfather's widow, gave the reception and I stayed with her before the wedding, with Hester in attendance. It was intended to be a small wedding and so it was difficult to ask everyone we would have liked, including friends and relations. Francis has a great many Chichester cousins, at least thirty-five first cousins, I believe. But in the end all went off beautifully. My two godsons, Robin Baker-White and Clive Foster, were pages. I should have liked to have Peter Thompson, my sister's eldest son, as well as these other godsons, but he wasn't young or small enough.

I'd always dreamed of a honeymoon in the sun, as many women do, I think. Not Francis. "Oh no," he said, "we must stay in England. And I don't want to go to an hotel, we must find a house." So a retired diplomat friend of mine very kindly offered me his small stately home, Newbiggin Hall in Cumberland. "If you take a cook up there with you," he said, "there's a married couple living there and you should be all right. It's shut up in the winter—do have it if you'd like to." I had already stayed there with him; it was a lovely house, and Hester good-humouredly agreed to come as cook.

When we duly arrived at Carlisle it was snowing. By that time we had become very fond of one another, Francis and I, and I knew that what I was doing was right. I felt this was my destiny without doubt and my life before had been a preparation for this; and I think Francis felt the same.

We were very happy together for a week there, and then within a week of coming south we went up to Tilbury and got on a New Zealand Shipping Line boat. It was practically empty. The great slump was on. But though there were very few other passengers aboard, we were very comfortable, it was beautiful weather, and we enjoyed the voyage via the Panama Canal. I was greatly looking forward to seeing New Zealand. My mother and father had been there on their honeymoon and had tried, unsuccessfully, to buy a farm. I had a very glorified picture of geysers and rainbow trout and a wonderful life altogether. Later I was somewhat disillusioned, but in fact my mother had also told me she was impressed at how frightfully hard the New Zealand women worked, and that she herself at that time did not even know how to boil an egg. She'd insisted on my taking cookery classes at Wantage, so in this at least I was reasonably well prepared.

Francis had been married before, when he was about twenty-two. I think he had realised even before they were married that they weren't right for each other. They were divorced and the child, George, stayed with his mother, but she died when he was only three. Now he was about eleven, and I thought it would be wonderful to have this boy to look after and give him a happy home life.

When we arrived at Wellington there were journalists waiting —it was my first experience of the Press. I landed full of hope, with a vast trousseau of beautiful clothes, most of them very unsuited for the life I was to lead living in a tiny house on the outskirts of Wellington, with limited means and having to do my own chores. I was embarrassed by the fact that when we married it was reported in the press that I was the granddaughter of a millionaire which in fact I was, but naturally they didn't say I hadn't inherited any of the money! When I got to New Zealand, the same thing appeared in the newspapers there, people expected me to entertain on rather a grand scale, and it was all very disappointing for them.

I am afraid I wasn't very adaptable at the time, and my outlook was very conservative indeed. Now, looking back, I realise I did learn a great deal from New Zealand, which leads the world in social reform. For example, it was while I was there that they initiated their health service, and I remember a certain amount of criticism of it among some people.

I tried to make the little house attractive with the furniture I had brought with me and one or two things I had made for me out there. Going back some thirty years later, I sat in one of the armchairs I'd taken with me from England. There was also a bed which I had had before I married—a marvellous bedhead with French chintz upholstery.

Francis seemed to be awfully depressed. He went through a phase when he'd only go out for walks in the evening and in the daytime sit about the house. I was extremely homesick and didn't write home to my friends. Some of them had doubted my suitability to go to New Zealand and I didn't want them to get the idea I had made a mess of my marriage already. I suppose that at heart I'm either very sophisticated or very simple; certainly when we got out into the bush I was frightfully happy. We used to walk for miles, camp, and swim in the most beautiful rivers. Francis was often busy fishing, which I wasn't so keen on, but this was something he enjoyed very much. These days out were marvellous, and it was only when I got back to the villa in Wellington that I felt very depressed and restricted again. I did, however, make friends with a delightful and brilliant German professor and his wife, Billie and Alice Von Zedlitz. She could have been my mother—they were married at the same time as my parents—and they really saved the day for me. I doubt if I could have stuck it out but for their kindness.

Then the day came to fetch my stepson, George, from his prep school. It was very touching how pleased he was to see a younger woman and to come to live with us. I always remember that I did a room ready for him and he said, "Is this my very own room?" which went to my heart. He had a very sweet nature but was awfully delicate and suffered from the most appalling asthma. This limited our lives very much; often we couldn't go out because George wasn't well and we couldn't possibly leave him. There was snow that winter, something the boy had never seen before. He rushed along trying to catch the flakes in his mouth and I thought this was rather enchanting.

Before a year was out, I decided I couldn't possibly stay in New Zealand. I couldn't see any future for us there. Francis had a forestry and real estate business with a partner called Geoffrey Goodwin. There was a slump on then and really there didn't seem to be anything in it for Francis at that time. It seemed to me that although he and his partner used to disagree a lot, they were really fond of each other. Coming back there thirty years later, we had a grand reunion, and I was amazed to see the wonderful forest which is now being milled and houses built all round it, a big community growing up.

War was coming in Europe and I didn't want to be out of my own country, so I said to Francis, "We'd better go back," and he agreed. I realised that he was a genius, but I thought he was wasting his talents out there and felt my work was really to look after him and build him up for what he was later able to do. After all, he'd lived half a lifetime of adventure before he ever met me—a most extraordinary career starting things up and letting them run down, making successful flights and smashing up his planes, this kind of pattern, and he'd never had any real support behind him. So we sold everything up. I had made some good friends there, particularly the Von Zedlitzs, and I was very sad to say goodbye to them; we all hoped to meet again in the future.

On the way back we went to Sydney. I immediately fell in love with Australia and I haven't changed my opinion of that country. We had a marvellous week there and a wonderful journey home. "We may never have another chance like this," I said to Francis, "let's just blow the money." So we went first class, taking George with us. We followed the route Francis had taken in his seaplane in 1931, and it was all a thrilling experience. We saw the Great Barrier Reef, Bali and various other islands, stopping off in Batavia, as it was called then; it's now

43

Djakarta. From here we took another Dutch boat, the *Christian Huygens*. Field-Marshal Von Blomberg and his wife were passengers on it, and also Victor and Victoria Plessen. Victor was an explorer and they'd just made a most interesting journey by canoe in Borneo. I remember Marshal Blomberg offered Francis a job in Germany, something to do with navigation in the Air Force, I think it was, but he didn't accept it.

In England it took Francis six months to find anything. No-one had an opening for him and we lived a worrying life in a furnished flat in London, wondering what on earth to do. Finally he got a job with Henry Hughes, the navigation specialists. Mr. Arthur Hughes was determined to have Francis and practically created a post for him. I don't know if the firm realised then how lucky they were to get him, but I for one have always been grateful to them. Francis started at ten pounds a week. My income continued, not a big one, just what I owed to my Craven grandfather's settlement, but this helped to carry us along.

The strange thing is that I never thought of taking a job then. Married women didn't. I just lived for Francis and planned everything for him. Every meal was thought out, we entertained a little, and I had a nice maid who used to come in by the day. We lived in Chelsea. I was very happy in this flat. We both were. George went to school, but though I spent a great deal of time trying to get him cured of asthma, taking him to various doctors and carrying out various treatments, I am afraid it was unsuccessful. It does seem to be my karma to have some ill person attached to me and needing to be looked after.

Then came the war. Francis tried to join the Air Force but was turned down on the grounds of eyesight. He tried to form a kind of suicide squad with Malcolm Douglas Hamilton, but nothing came of this. I volunteered for the WRAF and was interviewed by Miss Forbes who later became the Officer Commanding. I felt a bit scared because she said to me, "You'll probably be sent to all the danger spots." Little did I know then that I was to spend the whole of the war in London, working in the dock area all among the bombs and doodles and rockets, but this was something which just happened. In any event, the WRAF was off because when I told Francis he was horrified. "You're not to do it," he said. "I shan't be called up because of my sight and you will be in uniform and I shan't." "Oh very well," I said. I was relieved but ashamed that I did feel like that. Later in the year, at the time of Munich in the spring of 1938, I had the same mixed reaction even more strongly, and I remember speaking of it to Sir Sidney Barton when he came to dinner in our flat in Chelsea. My shame was that I knew we should have backed the Czechs and my relief because I feared the result of doing it. All the same, we didn't rush away from London at that time when many people did seem to be leaving and Harrods was very busy indeed moving household goods. Francis didn't want to go away and I wouldn't have gone.

But now war had come in earnest, and I sent my stepson George to the west country to be with his grandmother, Emily Chichester. Francis was continuing his work at Henry Hughes' factory, working on navigational instruments seven days a week. The lease of our flat came to an end and Mrs. Arthur Hughes invited us to stay with her in Chigwell Row. We did this for a time; she was extremely kind. Then we found a house nearby which was to be my home for the next few years. It was still in the London area but on the Essex side of it, near Ilford. Pages was a William and Mary House belonging to an eccentric lady who had lived there many years. She was loath to let us have it but finally agreed to a lease, and in the winter of 1939 we moved in. By now there had been all kinds of air raid scares, the carrying of gas masks and so on, but nothing much had happened. On one occasion I was out with Francis—he was having his early morning run—and an air raid warning sounded. The Warden appeared out of a shelter and told me, "Take cover, take cover." So I went towards a tree and at the same time some flak came down and just missed me. Later I discovered that this had come from some anti-aircraft guns at Ilford. A friend of ours was one of the officers there and he remembered firing at a plane they fortunately missed: it was a British one. It was all a case of early war nerves. There were months of tension but no fighting took place. My chief memory of this winter is how very cold it was and what heavy snow we had.

Then Germany suddenly struck, France was invaded. I remember going off on a visit with Francis to the West Country to find a factory near Bristol for Henry Hughes, Navigation Instruments. The work they did was very necessary to the war and in the event of bombing it was thought better to have another place in a safer area. The soldiers came flooding back from Dunkirk.

It was a frightening time; invasion seemed more than likely. In that May, when I was dining at the Café Royal with several journalists—Edward Ward was one, and George Steer, who later lost his life in Burma—they said the Germans were expected over tomorrow. But the Germans never came.

We returned from the West to Pages and stayed there. I joined up with Y.M.C.A. Mobile Canteens and worked for them till nearly the end of the war. Very heavy air raids started, London was in the front line and I watched it all. We used to see land mines floating down and landing all round us. I can remember the wild terror of the first air raids. Francis was blissfully happy. He dug a shelter in the garden and tried to get me out there. George by this time was back with us for the holidays. We had primus stoves in the shelter and all the things Francis loves tinkering about with. A local builder told me later that he wasn't at all satisfied with this shelter, that it was basically unsound and we should all have been squashed if anything had fallen very close to us. We had no gas or water for some weeks, there were all kinds of difficulties, but somehow we just went on and somehow we got used to it.

When the first air raid came I was driving my van in the docks. I was serving some soldiers in the Becton Gas Works when the siren sounded. "You'd better take shelter with us," they said. So I went in an air raid shelter with them and found it more frightening than staying above ground. I never went underground again after that if I could avoid it. There we all sat dying a thousand deaths, a sentry or sergeant or someone stood in the doorway and we made polite conversation. At last a long All Clear sounded and I have never felt more relieved.

As the raids grew worse I saw half the East End knocked down, because my route stretched from Dagenham to Bethnal Green, embracing the dock area. Rather foolishly I had put my car away feeling it wasn't right to use petrol when merchant seamen were being drowned. I served so many of them in the docks. Most other people kept their cars and I could have got an allowance of petrol, but anyway as it was I used to bicycle to our little station, Grange Hill, then take the train to Maryland and trolley bus to Plaistow where I collected my van. I can remember some terribly cold days and terrifying drives really, what with air raids, snow and ice and fog.

46

During this time our house was damaged eight times. After two years Francis went to the Central School of Flying in Wiltshire, and I longed for him to ask me to join him, but he didn't. He always said, "You'd better stay and hang on to the house." By that time we had in fact bought Pages, very cheaply. I lived alone there with my spaniels. When the flying bombs came, the house next door was hit, I was thrown out of bed, and all the ceilings came down: all this kind of thing which was familiar to so many people. When some soldiers were billeted on us, I thought that at least this would mean someone else would be in the house on these air raid nights. But not at all. When my sergeant arrived he told me that as soon as the siren sounded— sirene, they always called it—he had to go on duty as fire officer at the airport.

When D-Day came most of our troops left and the best trained people went overseas. So I was offered a job in an Officers' Club in Piccadilly also run by the Y.M. I decided to take this, though it meant more travelling into the centre of London and back, and it was quite an interesting job, very hard work. In August 1944 Francis came home on leave and said I ought to buy myself a house in London, we wouldn't want to stay at Pages. Off he went and came back declaring he'd found the right house. This was at the height of the doodlebugs and London was pretty empty. He brought me to 9, St. James's Place, I walked into this house and fell in love with it at once. Of course Francis is a very good salesman. He said to me, "There's a wonderful room will do for your drawing room, with three long windows and a balcony." And I pictured all this, as any woman would, and there indeed it was. In ten minutes I said, "Let's buy it." We went round to the Ritz and offered considerably less than was being asked, but in the whole of St. James's Place there were houses to let and for sale, and the street was practically deserted except for the Stafford Hotel, which was occupied by American soldiers. Not only did we get the house at our price but it carried a repair licence, which was considered a tremendous asset in those days; it also had some gas water heaters in the bathrooms, another great joy at that time.

So I set to work on the almost impossible task of getting a few things done to the house to make it habitable. Between working at the Officers' Club, looking after my sister who was

47

ill and keeping things going at Pages, I did all I could to get the place into some sort of order. My spaniel, Dimbleby, had to go with me wherever I went, and there were complications in crowded trains and buses. To help with the purchase price, we positively had to sell Pages. Everyone said it was in the bombing area and no-one would want it, but in fact it was sold to some friends at a price I had thought rather high. I felt I couldn't charge them that amount and said so, but they declared they'd always wanted the house and had the money and would pay it. My bank manager, who was always being gloomy about over-drafts and so on, had told me I'd never get this figure, but the curious thing is that I did get it, and Pages has since changed hands for quite a large sum.

In the spring of 1945 Francis arrived on leave and said we'd better move on. So we got a van, with great difficulty, loaded all our stuff in and arrived. I had my spaniel dog, and the bees, which Francis didn't want to leave behind, were put on the roof. By that time the rockets were falling thick and fast, but after a few weeks they stopped. Left alone in the house I remember feeling rather creepy. The top floors weren't occupied and I almost felt someone might be living there. By a great stroke of luck I was able to bring my telephone with me from Pages because that was in the London area too. But there were innumerable difficulties— you couldn't get laundry done, for instance—and there I was starting all over again to make something of this place. One of Francis's reasons for saying I ought to have a house was that he thought I could let it off in flats, which would give me an interest. We'd been married some years now and had no children. We had George with us, of course, and there was still this worry of his asthma. By this time he'd gone as an apprentice at De Havilland, but he wasn't awfully happy there and told me he would like to go in the Merchant Navy. I had always hoped he would go to learn forestry and be able to take over Francis's forest in New Zealand, and many years later he said he wished he had done this. But young people like to go their own way and I didn't wish to force him. I told him I thought the Merchant Navy was a good idea if he was keen on it, and why not try? So he had his interview, and, wonder of wonders, he had no asthma that day and was passed quite fit, in a higher grade than his friend who went up at the same time. He said, "I'm Grade A!" And I

48

Wren House, Kensington Palace. The Grace and Favour home of her great-grandmother, Mary Anne Thurston, nurse to Queen Victoria's children.

Mother and author in Sheila's first car, a Morris Cowley.

Sheila in a tennis dress
made by herself.

With friends holidaying in the
South of France.

Riding on Addis Ababa race-course.

said, "This is marvellous. You'll probably never have asthma again." He never did when he was at sea. He wouldn't become an officer, though they wanted him to, but went to sea in the catering department and was very, very happy. It was a great relief to me that he was enjoying life. He was in a French boat with British caterers and he told me the crew used to refuse to sail till they'd got their wine on board. They liked to live well, quite naturally.

V.E. Day brought great jubilations. I was still living alone that May but going often to see my sister, who had had the most dreadful sinus operations and suffered very much. I was worried about her health and always felt I'd failed her in not getting her fitter and happier in some way. My own problem was that now, having got the house, I had no income except a very small amount which was in trust for any child I might have. And it was a fairly big house to maintain and the rates had to be met. I set about advertising to let part of it. We had managed to furnish three floors. The basement was the dining room, with some nice furniture, including an oval antique Sheraton table I'd picked up very cheaply in the war. This room was all white, with white satin curtains. On the next floor Francis took a room for his office and his dressing room and bathroom, and the next one was my bedroom, bathroom and the drawing room. I managed to partly furnish one other floor.

The result of the advertisement was a letterbox bursting with requests which I had to cope with as best I could. First of all I let the top floor to a very charming couple. Meanwhile I was lumbered with a fairly big overdraft which was always a worry, and my experience of banks is that they aren't at all helpful to women. The truth was that I'd bought something which I really couldn't maintain. Francis always said he couldn't do much to help at that time and that he wanted to start a map-making business. And in those days I was no use as a business woman, though later I was to learn a lot and get much more with it.

The time came when Francis was demobilised and I went to join him in Devonshire. We had still very little furniture and he thought we'd better try to buy some. So we went round the antique shops down there and had a lot of fun. We found some nice pieces and it was well worth the difficulty of getting them to London. I enjoy house decoration and it was frustrating one couldn't do what one wanted. Still, it was possible to do a certain amount, and after we got back another flat was let to some very nice people.

Driving back from one of our visits to the West Country that autumn I suddenly noticed a heightened pleasure in everything. The trees looked more brilliant, the autumn tints and sky looked brighter, everything seemed marvellous. Later I connected this intense feeling of joy in living to the fact that I had become pregnant.

5

NATURALLY I was very pleased, but there were problems. I was determined to have my child born at home, which I believe is the proper place for a baby to be born. The conventional gynaecologist I was sent to said he never attended people of my age in a private house but only at the London Clinic or in a certain fashionable nursing home in Welbeck Street. His whole approach terrified me, and from the psychological point of view I was fascinated at the power this man seemed to have. "Of course, with the first child," he said, "the babies usually come all right. They do stick sometimes." I have never forgotten this remark and I fled from him.

At that time—and I am sure this was all fate—a very charming friend of mine, Grisel Stanley, who is a vegetarian and a mother of four children, had taken a room in our house to use when she popped up to London. When I told her about all this, "Oh, you must have Dr. Pink," she said, "he's the right man for you. He believes in natural childbirth and that the home is the right place to welcome the baby in." So Dr. Pink came to see me and I think he has been one of the greatest influences for good in my life. He was a priest as well as a doctor, a vegetarian, very gentle, very wise, and he used to come and talk to me, and from then on I was extremely happy. Dr. Pink did make me go down to his nursing home when he found that at five months I was cleaning the whole of the house and attending to my tenants. I had high blood pressure and he warned me that I might lose the baby if I went on like that. I had a week down there and calmed down, and also I learnt more about the vegetarian way of living.

The autumn before, Lord Cardigan had offered us a water bailiff's cottage on the River Kennet, near the south edge of Savernake Forest. There was a mile of fishing and also some rough shooting not far away. We were delighted to accept. The cottage had no drains, no water laid on—just a pump—and of course no electricity, but gradually we got things done and later we completed the conversion. When we left at the end of seven years it sold quite well. But at that time we used to drive down, Francis and I together, and our dog Dimbleby, and camp there. During the wintertime we would make marvellous blazing fires and were blissfully happy. Later on in the spring, Francis used to go fishing, which I am not so keen on, but I was content to hang about. We both loved it there. I couldn't get over the peace and the fact there were no terrible air raids to worry about. I also stopped worrying about money. I became a fatalist.

Then we came back to London, and at the end of July Giles was born. Very normally and perfectly in two hours, and I can truthfully say it was the most wonderful experience and happiest day in my life. Dr. Pink arrived exactly five minutes before the actual birth. One of my tenants upstairs, who was rather nervous and frightened, was convinced something was going to go wrong, but I had no such fears. After the child was born, I remember so well that my spaniel, Dimbleby, a dog I was devoted to, crept into the room literally on tip-toe, came and put his feet on the bed and looked at me. Of course if the nurse had seen she'd have been horrified, but after that the dog went and lay under the baby's cot and understood the whole thing. I've heard of cases where people have had to get rid of their dogs because they were jealous of a baby, and in fact, not having a child, I had, I'm afraid, lavished a great deal of love on my dog which, looking back, was probably wrong. But there was only trouble once, later on when Giles was about a year old and began climbing on to my bed, where the spaniel used to sleep. The dog went for Giles and caught hold of his arm. Giles went back at Dimbleby as if to bite him. It was most fascinating, because Giles had no fear and this dog never touched him again.

To make a nursery for Giles I had to turn out a very good tenant of mine, Anthony Bushell, the actor. I just asked him to let me have the flat back. It was a shame and again, I suppose, I was being very feckless about money, and Francis got very agitated about it. But later on we let this floor again. All in all, we were extremely lucky in the tenants who came to stay at No. 9, St. James's Place. Some of them have remained great friends ever since. Pauline Grant, the famous choreographer who does such wonderful work at Glyndebourne and Stratford, brought her mini-piano, which was a joy. Sir Garfield Barwick, now Lord

Chief Justice of Australia, once spent six weeks there. I thought he was one of the cleverest men I have ever met in my life. Also there was Pie Grimwade, a delightful Australian woman who was such fun and so gay and kind. Then there was the fascinating Siamese cat Anna, most beautifully behaved; she came to stay with her owner Villiers David while he was waiting to move into a new flat.

At the Christmas of that year we went down to the cottage. I stayed there till Giles was seven. It was a time of great learning for me, of development generally, I suppose, alone for the most part with this baby. Francis came back to London. Every corner of the house was by that time let but he kept one room for his office; he was starting up Francis Chichester Limited, Map and Guide Publishers. He used to come down to the cottage at week-ends, arriving on Saturday night very tired indeed. He used to sleep all day Sunday, and on Monday he went out shooting all day. It was rather lonely for me, but he felt desperately cooped up living in one room in London and needed this break of an out-of-door life. Giles was a wonderful companion as he got older.

I was a very strict vegetarian and at one time became a Vegan, but this made me so sensitive I decided it was more suitable for someone living in an Order, a monk or a nun. Throughout my life I have had direct signs given me, particularly with regard to religion. During this time I had been rather lukewarm and felt I couldn't go to Communion because I didn't really understand what I was doing. I daresay many people have these problems. Then one day a little child was taken ill in the village nearby. I was called in to help, but it had meningitis and I don't think it could have lived. This small girl's death was terribly tragic to the poor mother. I went to the funeral and the rector was a young man of such conviction that I felt a clear guidance that I must return to church. This rector became a great friend later; his name was Bertie Treasure. From then on I went regularly to the services in a little church on the hill. I consulted my friend Dr. Pink, telling him I found the sacrament of Communion a problem. "Very few people really understand what they are doing. You must just have faith," he said. After that I seemed to return to it quite naturally and have stayed that way ever since. I think that in Communion it is what you try to bring yourself which matters, and you receive help and the sharing of something with other people. At that time also I noticed that two of my greatest friends, persons I admired for their character and general stability, were both very religious women.

When Giles was old enough he wanted to come to church with me, and I was sorry that his father didn't come with us very often, but I think this is the case with many men. At this time I did feel rather cut off from Francis. Especially since I had become such a keen vegetarian, to see all this shooting and killing of game going on around was trying, but I had to make the best of it. It was difficult for Francis too, for men like to feel they're bringing home a nice pheasant for their wife to roast.

At the age of five, Giles went to a little morning school. A most charming lady who lived about five miles away took a few children; her motto was "We love to learn", and she really was wonderful with them. Giles enjoyed it very much. I think he loved this cottage of ours and, I hope, had a very happy childhood there. I felt I wanted him to have a natural life and it was a beautiful part of the country. When he was a baby I never drew his curtains at night, remembering how I used to suffer from claustrophobia and fear of the dark, and I used to show him the heavens and hope he would love the stars. I was passionately interested in them myself when I was six years old and bought a book about them with great pride. He used to go riding there, too, and in his early childhood he had peace and quiet all around him. But I don't think I really recommend husbands and wives splitting up like that. It is lonely for both, and you don't seem to see each other's point of view. This was very clear to me when I came back to London.

I really felt a stranger when I arrived. Some of the office people had taken over my lovely dining-room and I had to live in a part of the house which wasn't let. If somebody came along and wanted some rooms, I had to move into others. This also presented problems as to how to furnish them. I remember asking one wise old friend of mine, an interior decorator, how I should do up one flat. Francis always said my taste was so feminine I'd never get tenants. "Shall I furnish it in sort of male taste?" I asked her. "It always seems to be the men who come here. Leather armchairs and all that. . ." She said, "No, do it as you want it. And one day you might be lucky enough to live in it yourself." This was what I did, and the flat was let to a man who liked it so much he copied some features of it when he was doing up his own house in the country. I felt glad he liked the things I had, and if I remember rightly, by the time he left I was able to use part of this flat myself.

Just before we came to London, Francis telephoned me at the cottage one evening and said rather nervously, "I have bought a boat." It is a curious thing that most men seem to think their wives won't want them to have boats. (Perhaps they really like this feeling of not being allowed to do a thing; I don't know). I was absolutely delighted; I'd sailed long before I met Francis and it was beyond my wildest dreams to have a boat of our own. He was amazed when I said, "I've always wanted one." As soon as I came to town again, living in our rather cramped conditions, Francis started preparing the boat, which was up at Woodbridge in Suffolk. I immediately took an interest in her. This started off a really exciting chapter of my life, and in one way and another, the few years of quiet interlude I'd had in Savernake Forest were well and truly over.

6

THE NAME of the boat Francis had bought was *Florence Edith* until we changed it to *Gipsy Moth*. (*Gipsy Moth II;* the first *Gipsy Moth* was his plane.) It was a fairly cheap yacht and only a daycruiser, so it had to be converted for night sailing and offshore racing. Since Francis was so surprised by my enthusiasm over all this, I suppose I must never have told him much about the sailing adventures of my young days.

At the end of the First World War, my grandfather bought a very delightful property in the Isle of Wight for my aunt, Edith Kindersley. It was bounded on one side by Newtown River, now a very popular spot for yachtsmen, and there were about five hundred acres of fields and woods. The house itself stood up on the hill and looked over the Solent; it's called Hamstead and belongs now to her son, my cousin Dick Kindersley. When I was a child we used to go down to stay with my aunt—the one who later left me the legacy. We used to have a magical time and she was terribly kind to me. After my mother died she told me to look upon Hamstead as my home. I used to go swimming and sailing with her right up to the time she died, just before I met and married Francis.

I was a teenager when I started sailing there. My Uncle Archie had a yacht, quite a large yawl, and used to take us out with him. It was very different sailing in those days; he made us wipe our feet before going on deck and all was strict and proper. Occasionally I would be allowed to take a jibsheet, but for the most part what I liked best at the age of seventeen or eighteen was sunbathing and boyfriends, and of course Uncle Archie was more interested in sailing than in that sort of thing. But he liked girls around him, and he used to take me to tea on the lawn at the Royal Yacht Squadron at Cowes during Cowes Week, which was a very great event for me. I did enjoy those visits enormously, needless to say without the faintest notion that years later I would myself be a Lady Associate Member of the Squadron, have a very famous husband who sailed round the world, and that I myself would twice cross the Atlantic with him in our yacht. I had no thoughts of the future, I was just young and feckless, and I remember I made myself a very nice blue blazer and white pleated skirt. Only the other day I met a friend who said, "I've never forgotten how smart you looked at Cowes. None of us believed you when you said you made that outfit yourself." Many famous men and women used to come to Cowes in those days and there were the most beautiful yachts there, the great J Class ones with their billowing sails and vast crews. King George V was to be seen at the helm of his famous cutter *Britannia*. The royal yacht *Victoria and Albert* was in Cowes Roads and the King and Queen Mary used to land at the Squadron steps. I remember on one occasion having tea on the lawn with Lord Jellicoe; Lord Birkenhead was there too. It was quite another world, and there was a very sharp distinction between the yachting fraternity and the crowds that came and stared at them. It was very much a man's world too; ladies were not admitted inside the Squadron as they are today.

At first, though I longed to join Francis while he was trying out *Florence Edith* before she went into dock for alterations, I had no-one to leave Giles with and used to stay behind. But one weekend in November, Francis said, "You'd better come and have a sail in her," so I thought, "Why not?" A very kind friend of mine, Joy Matthews, whom I'd met at the Officers' Club in Piccadilly when we were both working there at the end of the war, invited Giles to stay for the weekend. I was given peremptory orders to be at the boat either by ten in the morning or six in the evening, and I said I'd meet him at six. I was to go to Brightlingsea on the East coast, a little grey town on an estuary with a very slippery seaweedy runway down to where the boats are. On the way there I had lunch with my cousin, Nancy Craven, who lived near Colchester. When I arrived at the jetty I enquired for *Florence Edith*, but no-one had heard of her, let alone Francis Chichester, no message had been left for me and although I went into the pub, where one can usually get the latest news, nobody knew anything about the boat.

Luckily for me, it was one of those wonderful warm November evenings. I went and sat on a bench and wondered what I should do, for I could see that fog was going to come down, and in those days we were short of money and I would have found it expensive to stay in an hotel for the night. Finally someone advised me to go to the Customs Shed and ask the Harbour Master about the *Florence Edith*. He knew nothing, but suddenly an old man (I don't know who he was) chipped in: "Oh, that boat," he said. "She be lying on her side on the Buxey"—a huge sandbank ten miles out to sea—"And what's more," he said, "it be lucky for her it's not rough or she'd be in a very dangerous position and there's thick fog coming. My advice to you is to go home. She won't be in till morning. If then," he added, "with this dreadful fog."

I must say I felt very annoyed. However, I had been on the mud when I was sailing with my uncle in the Newtown River, and I'd also seen other people doing it and knew it was something that could happen to anyone. Francis had always been a man who likes to find things out for himself and I didn't doubt there'd been an argument between him and the friend sailing with him about which side of the buoy to pass and they'd ended up on the wrong one. I telephoned my cousin who told me to go straight back to her house. By then I was a bit tired and agitated; it was thick fog, this was a part of the wilds I didn't know at all, and in those days I hadn't learnt to carry maps. However, after a slow crawl I did get back to Colchester and by great good luck, when I was just about deciding I'd have to spend the night in the car on a sort of common, a man on a motor bike came along. He knew the way from there to my cousin's house and I followed along after him, piloted by his little red light. So I arrived, and my cousin gave me a huge Martini and said I should divorce Francis for treating me like this. After a nice dinner with her I went to bed.

In the morning the telephone rang. My cousin, who has rather strong views about men, came in and told me, "Francis is on the phone. You give him hell!" What actually happened was that he said he was sorry, I said that was all right, he said, "Why don't you come for a sail?" and I said O.K. So off I went, my cousin declaring I was very foolish. But I'm pretty sure that had I not gone that morning, none of my exciting sailing career with my husband and son would ever have taken place, not in the same way, anyhow. I found Francis and Charles Colthurst quite easily and I think Francis had rather enjoyed the adventure.

He'd got out on the Buxey sand and had a long walk, leaving poor Charles, a more cautious type, sitting there wondering if the boat would come up all right, she was so heeled over. After floating off, they had made their way back to Brightlingsea in thick fog by the aid of a lead line.

We went for our sail and strangely enough for November, it was a glorious day. We even put our spinnaker up and it was flat calm. Perhaps we were still in the river, I can't quite remember but anyway it was very enjoyable. And when I got back to London, I found Giles had had quite a happy weekend, as I'd thought he would.

At this time Giles was going to a preparatory day school. I was rather criticised for not sending him away to boarding school, but I was quite determined I wouldn't do this, and Francis was against it too. After a great struggle I managed to get him a place at Westminster, which was very lucky because, apart from anything else, this school was so near our home. On the advice of the headmaster, John Carleton, a most wonderful man, I sent Giles as a weekly boarder, and I think this is perhaps one of the very best ways of education. I have seen friends of mine send away their sons when the children hated it. One little boy I can think of in particular has never been the same since. He was a charming, enthusiastic child. Next time I saw him he asked me to meet him and take him across London. He was a cringing, frightened little boy, terrified of losing his cap and absolutely different; they had all taken the mickey out of him. Francis always said that this had happened to him, and I think it is very curious that people send away their children so young. Giles benefited greatly from staying with his father, especially as he got older and Francis was more and more interested in him. I consider it was an important part of Giles's education living with a clever man like his father and meeting many clever people in our sailing world and business world. Of course, I think that there will be more and more mixed schools and that this will probably be much the best, with boys and girls growing up in a much freer way than we did. This is all to the good. Going to school in London, Giles had all his friends around him. There was never the problem you have in holidays from boarding school when the children have no natural playmates. In our case there were boys in the same street going to the same school as Giles.

They used to go off together to Westminster and it was a very happy arrangement.

In March the yacht was ready for sea. After that eventful weekend when I went to sail with Francis, I helped him to get her altered. We had the usual tussle with the designer who wanted to have his coach roof very low so that we shouldn't have been able to stand up in the boat. I had learned from my Uncle Archie that headroom was essential if you wanted comfort in a yacht, and I stuck to my point. Francis was glad of this later, when the yacht went in for fifteen or sixteen ocean races, always carrying a crew of five; not being able to stand up is hell. At this time I suggested advertising for someone to help us in the map business but also be available at weekends as a sort of mate. We got masses of replies and finally picked a very nice young man who seemed to know a lot about sailing.

One day at the beginning of March—it was one of those early Easters—Francis said he'd like to sail to Ostend for the weekend. Again I had the problem of my son, but I thought to myself, "Why not take him too?", because it is much more fun sharing everything. I've seen far too many families divided as a result of leaving the children behind on sailing expeditions. So off we went. It was frightfully cold and we had a perilous walk on to the boat over a rather ghastly plank. I am not very good at that, carrying stores and getting necessities on board. The last thing I asked for was a lifeline for Giles so that he could be secured to the boat. In those days nobody wore them; now, of course, it is standard practice and obligatory for an ocean racer to wear harness in the cockpit or working on deck. We set off down the river with a horrible wind blowing. I didn't know much then about winds or tides, but when we got to the river mouth it looked so rough that Francis said we'd better drop anchor and wait till morning.

Next day when we got out into the open sea the mate who was with us started to give me a lesson in sailing. "Look up at the burgee," he said, "Feel the wind on the back of your neck, or put up your finger and wet it and you'll see which way the wind's coming." Well, this mast looked awfully high to me and immediately I began to feel very sick, so I retired below. I'd brought along a little champagne for myself and also some brandy, to be on the safe side, but neither of these was any good and I was sick. Giles was too; I don't remember whether the others were. Anyway, night fell and I lay on my bunk feeling scared and deathly cold. In the hurry I hadn't got the proper clothes, or I shouldn't have been so frozen. Before we set out Francis had taken me down to Gardiners, a shop in the City for yachting equipment, and fitted me out in men's oilskins. They were so heavy and so uncomfortable I felt imprisoned in them. "God help me," I thought, "if I fall overboard." Giles flatly refused to come below for the night and stayed in the cockpit. I made sure he was attached by his little lifeline and had rugs tucked around him, and there he stayed.

In the morning we arrived at Ostend, which was quite exciting except that the tide was out and we ended up sitting right down at the bottom of the dock with a ghastly iron staircase to climb up. I didn't like the look of it at all, but the mate, who was a staunch Catholic, having given one a little pep talk on being smart for the sake of morale, dressed himself up and disappeared to go to Mass. So I thought to myself that I wasn't going to let the side down and decided I'd find out where the English church was and attend the service this Easter Sunday. Giles and Francis didn't wish to come but I climbed those awful steps and made my way to the church. It was a lovely service. I was still cold and was glad to kneel by the stove. When I spoke to the Chaplain he was quite impressed to hear I'd arrived by water in a small yacht. This was fifteen years or more ago, remember. There was still rationing in England, so I bought a lot of butter. We had some excellent meals and quite a lot of fun, though the weather remained rough and very cold. I looked at a lot of trippers going off in a crowded steamer for home and I envied them and wondered whether I shouldn't go too with Giles. But I hadn't really enough money with me to pay the fare, nor did I want to opt out. A very nice Belgian pilot said to me, "Oh madame, I have just been out and there are big waves. Please ask your husband not to take you tonight to sea with your little son." When I mentioned this to Francis he became quite annoyed. He was determined to go that night, and also to leave at night, for he loves night sailing. Now I know more about it I'm sure he's right to leave in the dark and arrive, if you can, by daylight wherever you're going. Anyway, we set forth and by that time I decided I would take a seasick pill. I was roused from a heavy sleep hearing us bump and go aground and I thought, "Oh good, we shall stick now." But it was a rising tide and off we went. Giles and I lay prone in our bunks.

When I woke up we were in the North Sea, wallowing past a light vessel. I went into the cockpit and began to appreciate sailing and to enjoy it. Eventually we ended up in Woodbridge where the yacht had been built and managed to get off although we went aground and heeled right over on our side, which was very uncomfortable. And somehow I also managed to keep awake and drive the three sleeping males back to London. From then on I always went sailing with the boat and Giles did too, for being at a day school meant he was free to go with us at weekends. We started on a very strenuous time of ocean racing. Like all beginners, we had to find out the hard way. Francis, of course, always likes to experiment; he thinks this is the best way to learn, and he is probably right. He had already become a member of the Royal Ocean Racing Club, a mixed club where women can be members in their own right, so of course my next ambition was to join this distinguished club.

Francis had planned to go on the Corunna Race that summer and I meant to sail back with them from Spain. However, this was not to be; they were dismasted and got no farther than the Channel Islands. Francis telephoned suggesting I should join him there for a little cruise. My plane to Guernsey was delayed by bad weather and no-one was there to meet me when I arrived, but walking along the front at St. Peter Port, I suddenly bumped into Francis. This is typical of the sailing life. We stayed on board while the boat was being repaired. Living on a boat without a mast is extremely uncomfortable; however, I got used to it. Then one day we set off for Dinard. That was a lovely sail. We arrived there in bright moonlight, with the moon making a great band of silver on the water. There were countless flashing lights and buoys ringing bells and so on, for this is a very dangerous bit of water to navigate. We ended up in the Bassin Vaubin at St. Malo. What a lovely place it is—an old walled town with marvellous restaurants! Several other yachts were there and we made some new friends. Francis sent our crew away because he wanted me to get used to sailing alone with him, so after a day or two at St. Malo we sailed by ourselves to Iles Chausey, a heavenly spot where we spent a day bathing and swimming and sunbathing.

Next day it was quite plain there was a big storm coming, but we started off nevertheless and managed to get to Jersey, where we were stormbound for five days. This is a very awkward place to be stuck in because the tides go up and down so that you spend your entire time rushing back to adjust warps. There's not enough water for the yacht to float at low tide. I shall never forget the fury of the wind and seas there, and all the trippers marooned. No planes were flying, the boats came in overloaded, and it was all rather grim. Francis insisted on staying aboard and I was worrying about Giles. On the fifth day Francis said, "We must go."

Although the storm had abated, when we got outside it was like being on one of those switchbacks at a fair. While we were plunging up and down Francis asked me to take the helm. Only one thing cheered me up. I suddenly looked and standing out on the skyline were two great sailing ships, square-rigged. I learned afterwards that they were training ships on their way to America. After a night at St. Peter Port we went on to Cherbourg. I was very frightened of the Alderney Race, but we sailed through with the tide with us—flat calm, and we went at about 12 knots; very lovely and exciting weather. We arrived a bit late and I was pretty tired after all these agitations, but we went into town and had a marvellous dinner in a restaurant there. On the way back, about ten o'clock, I was looking round me as usual, fascinated by the fishing boats in the harbour, when I slipped and fell. I heard a nasty crack in my ankle and felt terribly faint. However, Francis pulled me up and people crowded round saying, "You must get up, you must get up! We're going to raise the bridge." Evidently I'd fallen on the part of the bridge which joined the road and they were pulling it up for the boats. Making me stand up like that was the last straw and I fainted. I came round to hear Francis saying, "Elle est morte," and a girl echoing him, "Oui, oui, elle est morte." When he saw me moving, he went for me—I suppose he'd had a dreadful fright—and said, "You've had a stroke." I was a bit shattered at this, but I didn't think one usually came to like that after a stroke. My ankle was very painful indeed, but I bandaged it up with a silk scarf and said I was all right. A taxi had come along and the driver offered to take me to a doctor but I thought, "No, I'd rather get on our own boat." I insisted on having the taxi, however, although it was only a very short way; I don't think I could have walked it. Somehow I got on board. We sailed next evening and it blew up very rough that night. I'd hurt my wrist as well as my ankle in the fall. It was so painful to take the helm that at last I said to Francis that I really must lie down. We got to Yarmouth the following morning, and I remember the beauty of being in mid-channel and Francis showing me the loom of the light at Cherbourg and the loom of the light at Needles, but on the whole it all seemed pretty rough and unpleasant to me.

We arrived in Yarmouth flying the yellow flag. In those days not all that many people went abroad in their boats and so it was something of an event. Friends brought us cups of tea and I hobbled to the telephone and stood in a queue to ring my sister. Giles was staying with her, we were late owing to this rough weather and I had missed his birthday. Kathleen seemed a little fussed and said to hurry back at once. She couldn't keep Giles any longer, and what with one thing and another I felt rather desperate. However, we set out and got back into Beaulieu River, travelled up to London by train and arrived by midnight. When I saw a doctor he sent me off for an X-ray. It turned out I'd broken a bone in my ankle and also torn the big ligament. Which shows what the human body can stand: that bone was broken on the Saturday and it was not set until the following Tuesday afternoon. Francis was quite amazed; he had had no idea I'd hurt myself so badly. I was sad because I'd just ordered a new car and now I was to be immobilised for six weeks and wouldn't be able to drive it. Still, there it was. Francis went off on another race, Giles and I stayed at home, and during this time my son was so good to me, looking after me and helping in every possible way.

The following season I decided to try and join the R.O.R.C. and set off on the Dinard race, which is a ladies' race. We left in brilliant weather, but after we got past St. Catherine's down came a thick fog and we sat with horns hooting all round us until we came quite near to Dinard. Then it lifted completely and we had a lovely run down under a spinnaker. I remember friends greeting us when we got there. We were about the last boat in, but honestly, if I'd been the first person to cross the Channel I couldn't have been more thrilled and happy. There was a nice dinner that night, and later on we attended a prize-giving.

These original designs brought Sheila the offer of a job in Paris.

Mobile canteen in the London Docks during 1939-45 War.

9 St. James's Place, London.

I was full of admiration for those who won cups and very much hoped I might be lucky enough to do so one day. And in fact this did happen a year or two later, when we won the cup for the A Division boat.

Just one more of my earlier sailing experiences comes very vividly to mind, partly because it was one of my most frightening passages and partly because Giles was involved. My son and I were due to join Francis at Belle Ile at the end of the San Sebastian race. We had a strenuous journey, ending up by taking a little ferry boat to the island through rough seas. Poor Giles was sick, I just managed not to be. We both felt ghastly when we got there, and as yet no sign of Francis. The Commodore of the club at Belle Ile met us and kindly took us to some rooms for the night. These were in one of the creepiest houses I've ever been in. The lights kept going out, but I had a torch and somehow we got to bed. The bigger boats started coming in next morning. We hung about Belle Ile and finally Francis and Co. arrived. The weather was so rough we had to wait and in the end the rest of our crew went off, leaving Francis, myself, Giles and Stormy Nicol (a well known ocean racer and a fairly regular member of our crew) to get the boat home. We left with a very bad weather forecast but Francis seemed frantic to get away. I could never argue with him and he just sailed. A friend of ours, a yachtsman who saw us leave, said, "That man wants his head looking to, sailing with a wife and child aboard." In this way we were pioneers; people take their children now as a matter of course, and Dr. Lewis, for instance, thinks nothing of having toddlers as passengers in the Straits of Magellan in his catamaran *Rehu Moana*.

It soon blew up very, very nasty weather. We were out in the Bay of Biscay, water was coming over, and I felt very sick. Giles started being sick every few minutes, which worried me very much; it is bad for a child of only eight. So Francis said, "Really I ought to stand out to sea tonight with this weather, but if you like I'll try to get in. I could go to Concarneau or Benodet." I'd always wanted to go to Concarneau, it sounded to me such a lovely little place. "Let's go to Concarneau," I said. Looking back, considering the charts, and the rocks he had to bring us in through with this terrible weather and visibility, I wonder if I shouldn't have said, "Let's stay out at sea all night"; really it would have been safer. However I've always had great confidence in Francis's powers of navigation provided he is not interfered with, and we made it. The seas were running so high the whole place seemed swollen. We were wet through and through. Giles was marvellous; I did admire the child. His father said to him, "Giles, you've been a very good boy. I'll give you five bob to buy some soldiers." Giles promptly said, "Ten bob," so he wasn't as ill as all that. We were feeling absolutely exhausted when we got in, but we'd barely come into port—such is the resilience of children —before Giles was saying he was hungry, so up we had to get and prepare a meal.

Next day I went ashore and told Francis I was going to leave him and Stormy Nicol to bring the boat up to Dinard; Giles and I would meet them there. I felt Giles had been through enough and it wasn't fair to him. By great good luck I not only got a nice room in an hotel but a bathroom too. "Very extravagant to have a bathroom," Francis said. I went out for a walk. When I came back, to my great amusement, there in my hotel bedroom was Stormy Nicol lying on the bed, and Francis in the bath, very happy. They went off after an excellent dinner. Next morning I saw them from the window, plunging about, and was thankful to be in our comfortable hotel. There was no *Gipsy Moth* when we got to Dinard but after a while they appeared. I think they'd spent the night near some breakwater off Ushant. Stormy Nicol had to get back to his office, so he departed. I've never seen him so tired out; he just sat on the edge of his bunk and hardly spoke. As for the three of us, it was a ghastly business getting into St. Peter Port when we finally reached it; people watching us said they were thinking of sending out the lifeboat. The wonderful steward at the Channel Islands Club dried our clothes, we had drinks and everyone was terribly nice to us. Finally Giles said, "I want to fly home, Mummy, I don't think I can go on." I said, "Neither can I, Giles; I'm fed up." Although Francis said we were disgusting to desert him and were a rotten crew, I stuck to my point that we must leave the boat. There are times when one must be disciplined and admit defeat.

Later on, Francis and I and a very charming and brilliant yachtsman called Marston Tickell came back to St. Peter Port and had a wonderful sail back in the autumn. It was calm weather and a nice wait in Cherbourg and, as they had promised, they woke me at dawn to see the Needles in the pale daylight with the moon waning and the lighthouse beam turning. There are moments when every unpleasant thing in sailing is wiped right out and you know it's all worthwhile. Marston Tickell was a splendid man to sail with, a good comrade and so encouraging. He even said he thought perhaps he was unlucky never to have been seasick because afterwards you must feel so well. I thought this a very generous way of looking at it.

7

UNFORTUNATELY all this sailing had not been too good for Francis. He had tried to do too much. Any skipper navigator in a small boat with an inexperienced crew— and though we had some very nice people to help us, few of them had much experience—is bound to get exhausted. In 1955 after the Dinard Race, we had got to St. Malo and the crew had gone home when Francis became very ill, the first of the extraordinary illnesses he was to have over the next two years. He seemed now to lose the use of his hands and was in great pain with his shoulders. It appeared to be arthritis. I thought to myself, "Here we are again, worrying about Giles back in England, again a birthday pending, and Francis absolutely unable to leave his bunk, almost crippled." I got a French doctor who said my husband was "tres fatigué" and prescribed some pills which turned out to be butazolidin, a very strong drug. In the night Francis was quite delirious. I don't like drugs, I was alone in the yacht with him, and I was worried and desperately wanted to get him home. He stopped taking the drug after that. I persuaded him to leave the boat there, and the Harbour Master was splendidly helpful, promising that if we gave a small fee to the club man he would keep an eye on *Gipsy Moth* and it would be quite safe; the only danger really would have been from the English trippers. I was lucky again in getting a cabin on the *Falaise*, but Francis was in great pain all the way.

Nevertheless, after a few days he insisted on going back for the boat and putting her in for the Fastnet Race, which he had always wanted to do. Just before this, Giles was seized with an emergency appendix and had to be rushed into hospital; I think the operation took place literally on the Friday before the start of the race. When Francis had rung up the previous night I told him Giles was fine and not to worry, for there was nothing he could have done anyway and I wanted him to enjoy the race. So they went off and just missed by twenty minutes getting the Aurelius Plate, which is the prize for A class boats. I think *Gipsy*

Moth missed it mainly because a marine joining the crew had brought a very heavy suitcase and stowed it under the counter while we were fussing around Giles and his appendicitis; this must have added an enormous amount of weight to the yacht. Having completed the Fastnet, Francis came off looking terrible, his face all swollen and so on, and he left the yacht at Plymouth and came home. It was quite plain he was very ill and I felt something must be done about it at once.

By this time Giles had come out of hospital, a bit shaky after the operation, and our doctor suggested Francis should go down to Edstone, a nature cure home near Stratford-on-Avon. Giles and I joined him after a while, and Giles camped in the heavenly grounds there; we had a very happy time. Francis gradually got better but he was very, very weak then. He had this curious arthritic condition and could hardly lift a tea-cup to drink. But I was determined he should not have any gold injections or any of that type of treatment; that he could and would be cured by natural methods. I had seen my mother absolutely devastated by the effects of orthodox medicine and die in great pain, and I was determined the same thing should not happen to my husband.

Francis was worrying about the yacht. It was time to lay her up for the winter and Mashford's Yard at Cremyll was full. I went down there and pleaded with Syd Mashford to take her. Giles was with me; he had had an accident while we were on our way from London and was hopping along on one leg. The other had been stitched up at a Plymouth hospital after he had got a spike right through his calf. He was doing a commando act on some iron railings while we were staying at a friend's house near Plymouth. Syd Mashford finally said, "Well, I can't refuse women and children, I must help you. I will keep your boat." This started a firm friendship with that wonderful yard and those wonderful brothers, and *Gipsy Moth* was put to bed at Plymouth.

Meanwhile, before this, I'd said to Francis, "You really must get yourself a decent boat. It's time you did." I could see what a brilliant navigator and seaman he could become with a proper boat, but pushing this old thing along was really an awful strain on him. And so it came about that Robert Clark designed *Gipsy Moth III* for us. Little did we know the trials and tribulations we were to have before this boat was launched and how famous she would become afterwards, but most good things come out of suffering and hard work. Most of the interior of that boat was laid out in our drawing room. We planned and plotted and Robert visited us and we had a tremendous lot of fun that winter. Francis recovered from this arthritic condition, though his general health still seemed to be deteriorating. Curiously enough, an osteopath who saw him at this time advised him never to go back to a sporting life. I must add, however, that when this man knew Francis had won the Trans-Atlantic Solo Race, he sent us a very marvellous letter and said he was sorry he had told Francis this.

In the Fastnet Race of 1957 Francis went as navigator in a famous ocean racer called *Figaro*. She belonged to Bill Snaith. It was very rough weather, one of the roughest Fastnets they have had. Like many busy American yachtsmen, Bill had to fly home and have his yacht shipped back to America, and to do this she had to be sailed from Plymouth, where the Fastnet ends, to the Port of London. He asked Francis if he would sail her up with Bucky Reardon, the sailing master, and Ted Robbins, a student, two young Americans who were on board as crew. Francis asked if he could take me too and Bill said, "Yes, certainly."

We went down to Plymouth to join the yacht which was lying in the Mill Bay Dock, and left when the gates opened at three in the morning. There was a pretty fresh breeze blowing—I should think it was 6 or 7—but we were running dead before and had a splendid run up the Channel averaging 7 knots. By about four in the afternoon we were off St. Catherine's in the Isle of Wight. I had been secretly hoping that they would go into the Solent and spend the night at Cowes as I could see we were in for some extremely rough weather. Francis, who was navigating, had retired as he often does and was having a sleep. One of the boys said to me, "Do you think he knows where we are?" I was somewhat amused because I know Francis's habits well: when he wants to have a rest he leaves people knowing they are in a safe position and we had plenty of sea room on this occasion.

The weather got progressively rougher and rougher until it was for me the most terrifying storm I had been in up to that time. All that night we ran up the Channel under bare poles. I remember that, just after we left the Isle of Wight, Francis advised taking down the trysail and as they took it down it sounded like a whip cracking. There was nothing much I could do so I got into my bunk hoping for the best. It really was a terrible night. Our lights failed and Bucky kept putting up a little oil lamp. I know it was to keep me company—Americans are so kind—but invariably it blew out as soon as he got it up. Next morning when I woke up and looked out, "Goodness," I said to Francis, "how green the cliffs look!" "Don't be silly," he said, "those are waves you're looking at."

By this time we were off Dover and I was thankful they decided not to press on to London but to put in there. Just as we were trying to get in the inevitable happened—they closed the gates of the Dock. "Oh dear," I thought, "we're going to be plunging about outside again." But luckily we were able to get into another place which had been a submarine pen in the war, and there we gladly dropped our anchor. We were terribly cold and hadn't even the heart to go ashore for a meal. However, next morning after a good night's rest, we sailed on up to London. It was interesting to see the rough seas and all the people trying to have their holidays on the crowded beaches. After various adventures we arrived in the Thames. Trying to bring a yacht into the Port of London at night is like trying to find a place in a crowded car park. No-one seemed to want us but finally we managed to get into a quiet backwater and tie up. I remember someone saying, "Oh I would like a drink" and someone else saying, "You can't have one. Sheila's asleep against the liquor locker."

The sailing master, Bucky Reardon, was awfully worried about rats. In America you had to have a special certificate to the effect that your boat had been cleared of rats; we don't have such a thing in this country. To my horror a man passing by next morning called out to me, "That's a lovely little boat of yours, but for goodness' sake don't have a line to the shore or you'll get rats on board." I thought poor Bucky would have a fit, but in the end we dropped an anchor and all was well.

One of my memories of that night (and it is always the same in big storms at sea in a yacht) is the terrible noise and screaming of the wind and crashing of the waves on the side of the boat.

I asked the two American boys to come and stay with us while they were in London. We made great friends and in America in 1960 when I was waiting for Francis after the first Solo Race and desperate to know how to get some kind of craft to go out to meet him, Ted Robbins and his wife came up to New York, looked after me and helped me to find a boat, so this was a very happy result of our meeting.

That winter of 1957 my husband became very ill with bronchitis, pneumonia and goodness knows what. After Christmas he had X-ray tests which showed a most unusual condition (proved not to be tubercular) superimposed on a sub-acute asthma. He was advised to attend a famous clinic at a London chest hospital, and because he was determined to have treatment on the National Health scheme, it meant long hours of waiting. They try to do too much for too many people with too few people to do it; the time just isn't there. One day after he'd had an X-ray he was called into the leading surgeon's room and to his amazement was demonstrated to twelve doctors and students. The surgeon said to them, "This man is an example of an advanced case of carcinoma." He told Francis to hold out his hands for the inspection of this audience and so on. Francis came back and described all this to me and asked me what the word "carcinoma" meant. It was amazing that he didn't know, but I was well aware this is the medical term for cancer. I am afraid I was filled with fear but turned firmly to prayer, always believing he was going to get well.

On March 19 our doctor telephoned and asked me, "Are you alone?" I said yes, I was, and he went on, "Well, they've examined the X-ray and they fear it's an early growth in the lung." I said, "What is the best thing to do?" He replied, "Go on nursing him with great care and patience. Look after him all you can." I did my best, tried to prepare tempting food and salads and things he liked, but it was hard going—he was obviously very ill. They then advised him to have a bronchoscope which is to say that an instrument is put down your throat and they look inside your lung. When Francis had had this done he rang me up and said the man who'd made the examination had told him it was carcinoma of the left main bronchus. "He could see the growth there," my husband told me, "and he thought it was probably too late to operate." Then there was a long wait while they did a biopsy. Privately, a man assured Francis the result was negative, but I don't understand this because immediately they said an operation was necessary. However, I have been told that you can have a growth which is dormant and some doctors think it wise to remove it.

72

Throughout all this time I was horrified at the state of fear to which they'd reduced Francis. I continued to keep as cheerful as I could, always believing and playing for time and praying that no operation would be necessary. Guided by some inner force, I had clear knowledge that this operation must not take place. For nearly five years before all this happened, I had been attending lectures on healing. Every Wednesday a friend of mine ran a class in Harley Street; all kinds of people addressed us and my own instinctive faith in natural recovery had been greatly strengthened. I also attended regular services at Church where we prayed for sick people and received much help and encouragement from our rector and other friends.

On April 9 an operation was advised. The growth had been categorically diagnosed as carcinoma by eminent specialists, one a leading surgical chest consultant in London. This opinion was given in writing, in two letters which our doctor has. Francis agreed to have the operation and booked a bed, again on National Health. When he came back and told me this, I said it was mad and that if he was determined to have the operation, was he at least sure a top surgeon would perform it. "The big chief probably won't be able to do it," he said. He seemed obsessed by this "big chief" idea. These surgeons are very brilliant men and they obviously wield tremendous power. However good many of them were, I still felt that it was better to hang on to your lung rather than have it cut out. However, I said to Francis, "Why don't we try to find the best private surgeon in London?" So we went to another doctor who reduced me to tears by telling me Francis's was the most shocking case of neglect. He didn't like nature cures, obviously. And I remember he said to me, "Can you pay?" I answered that of course one can pay if one has to, frantically wondering where the money was to come from but having faith. So this doctor said he'd book Francis in at the same hospital in a private ward and proposed as his surgeon Mr. So-and-So, naming the same man who'd been attending Francis at the National Health Clinic. These surgeons do some operations on the National Health but they also have private patients; obviously they couldn't survive financially if they didn't.

I think that deep down in my heart I had always been determined Francis wasn't going to have this operation, but I was under great pressure from everyone. The nature cure doctor was on my side. He told us very frankly that according to the statistics of this particular operation, only ten per cent of cases were successful. This man was a surgeon before he turned to nature cure, so I suppose you might say he was an orthodox medical man turned unorthodox. Although he had seen some wonderful operations, he had also seen recovery without them. And in any case, Francis was so ill at this time that I was certain the operation would kill him. Even apart from this fear, the idea of him without a lung seemed terrible to me, like cutting off a bird's wing. He had so liked flying and going out on the ocean. I asked then to see this surgeon, and when I explained I would pay for the consultation, this was arranged. By now Francis was in hospital, in a semi-private ward with two other men. When I took him there I was very frightened because one of these patients had just had this same operation. He was lying on his bed absolutely snow-white, stuck about with all sorts of tubes, and an Indian doctor was leaning over him, which made him look all the whiter. Later I made friends with this man and he was so charming, apologising for having given me such a fright.

The day came for me to see this great surgeon. I was scared to be opposing the decision of this very eminent man, but I could not change my destiny. I told him I felt the operation was unnecessary. He got very impatient with me and said, "You are the most extraordinary woman and you're wasting time." I said, "I apologise, I realise you're a busy man." He'd come out after one operation and was going back to do another. He said, "No, I mean the patients' time," and went on to assure me that a lot of people lived quite safely with one lung. But I stuck to my point and he agreed to make another examination of Francis. So I thought, "Well, I've gained time, he's not going to be cut up." And the surgeon and I said goodbye. I went to see Francis and he thanked me for what I had done.

Meanwhile the doctor who had sent us privately to this surgeon went on holiday and another one came. I regard all this as a train of events. In some curious way it was fate that this different doctor took over. Well, Francis had another bronchoscope, this time under an anaesthetic. Though I never saw this surgeon again, nor did he send me a bill for my consultation, the operation did not take place. However, Francis still lay in this hospital,

74

looking so dreadful and despondent, so thin. I used to go to see him every day. It was the time of the big bus strike and I'd sold our car earlier that year because it was impossible to park it in our street. So now I either had to go on the Underground, which I disliked, or walk. I did try hitchhiking but very few people stopped—usually people with shabby old cars. The limousines flashed past. This is life, I suppose. Besides going every day to talk to Francis, I sent two friends of mine who are priests, but both worried him. I think he was suffocated by religion as a boy. Some time before, I had met a Jesuit Father, a very delightful man, who was writing a book on the lives of early navigators, and I remember saying to him, "Why are you doing this?" He answered, "You see in ancient times my Order used to go with the ships because we were the only ones who could read and write." I had a sort of feeling this man might be the right one to help Francis, and though I didn't ask him at that time, later on when my husband recovered, I said, "Would you like to see Father Kelly?" and he said, "I believe I would." That Father Kelly was a Roman Catholic and Francis had been brought up as a Protestant didn't seem to me to have the least significance. I believe that religion is undenominational and I shall continue to do so. During Francis's illness, friends who were Christian Scientists, Catholics, Protestants, all sorts and kinds of people prayed for him. This was very necessary and helped towards his cure.

This was a sad time for me. The house seemed dark and empty of life. Luckily, I had Giles with me for company. I tried as much as possible to keep all this from him. It is not good for children to see such illness. He was only a schoolboy, and even as it was they knew from his work that he was in a disturbed state and had wondered what had gone wrong in our home life until I explained how things were. For my own part, I felt I was fighting a strange battle, but I kept steadily on my course. I prayed a great deal. Every evening when I came out of the hospital, I used to sit in St. James's Park for a while. It was lovely there, and looking at the flowers and birds I longed for Francis to be well and share all this again.

The weeks moved on and finally the hospital said it was time for Francis to leave. By then no-one ever really seemed to know what was the matter with him. There were endless tests and

X-rays going on, but I asked them not to use any more drugs, and the junior doctor there was very helpful to me. He was an understanding person. The nurses, too, really cared for their patients and looked after them wonderfully. I must confess I felt a total lack of communication with the doctors in general. I very rarely saw any of the senior doctors, and I fear I must have seemed a very strange individual, always questioning what they were doing. But they were very patient, and though I felt in a curious vacuum of frustration, I did not lose heart.

After a while I decided I would try to get Francis away to the country, and so it was that he came to a hydro called Enton Hall. This Hall at one time belonged to some cousins of his, and I felt that back in an old Chichester home he might recover his strength. Unfortunately he decided after a fortnight that he'd take a hut in the garden to save money. It was very, very cold and undoubtedly he caught a severe chill. He became very ill again and had the most appalling asthma. But he fasted, I went down whenever I could possibly leave the house and the business, and always I prayed. During this time I myself received the laying on of hands on his behalf. This can be helpful; I was the nearest person to Francis, and this power can be transmitted.

Finally, one day when I went to the clinic Francis seemed to have gone back terribly and the people there said to me, "We really can't keep your husband any longer; we're not used to nursing anyone who's as ill as he is." I asked our nature cure doctor Gordon Latto to come down and he said Francis's heart was being affected. "Do hot and cold packs," he told me. This is hydrotherapy which they practise a lot. Then they all left me and I stayed with Francis. Everything seemed pretty terrifying that night. I felt this was a crisis. He was frail and very ill, on a thin edge. So I remained there; they were extremely kind to me at Enton Hall, letting me have a room whenever they could, though I was always having to hop from one to another because they were so full.

Next morning he seemed a little better and then slowly, slowly he seemed to pick up until he was absolutely well, able to walk to the village. Throughout this I always said to him, "You must get well because of your new boat." I felt a complete certainty that he had a lot more to do in the world, for himself and for other people. And later this proved true in his splendid passages across the Atlantic, his circumnavigation and his opening up of communications on small yachts. Meanwhile Giles and I used to come to visit him, and it was only once, when he got a little bit of asthma again, that he wasn't still improving. One wonderful day I hired a self-drive car, we drove him home and got him back.

The following April Francis decided to go down and visit his family in Devonshire. He was a bit shaky still but, on the whole, gaining strength. He'd got into the habit of having oxygen in his room and took this whenever he felt a suffocating feeling. One Friday my sister-in-law telephoned to tell me Francis was very ill again and that she'd had to call the doctor. "What does he say it is?" I asked at once. "Cancer," she said. I knew they didn't believe he had really recovered. "Don't talk such nonsense, he's got no cancer now. Let him rest, leave him alone," I said, "and then as soon as he's strong enough he'll come back." All this I remember very vividly; it was on my birthday, April 11. When Francis returned to London, I told him I thought he had better face up to going for another X-ray. "Supposing there is anything in it," he said. "There won't be," I said with complete confidence. "I'm sure of it." At this time I'd arranged for Giles to go on a visit to France with some other schoolboys and we had been thrilled planning this for him. I was so glad he was going to get away and have a little fun after all this illness; he had been wonderful to me, my son. When Francis came back "Everything's all right," he said, "I've got absolutely clear lungs. I want to go to France too." So I saw Giles off with his knapsack along with the rest of the school party and then we dashed off ourselves to the south of France.

We went first to a place near St. Paul which I rather liked. I enjoyed looking out of my window at the moon and seeing the beautiful silhouette of this lovely old walled town. But Francis was miserable there, it didn't seem to suit him at all, so we moved on to another hotel in Vence. Here he was quite happy until, after a day or two, he was taken awfully ill again. We had to walk back to the town a few steps at a time and then he would lean against a tree; he couldn't get his breath and it was terrible. I thought, "Can I stand much more of this? Am I wrong?" Yet at some deeper level I knew it was going to be all right. Francis said he must have oxygen; I think he had come to use it as a sort of escape. We found that in France you cannot have oxygen supplied by a chemist without the consent of a doctor, so I thought, "Oh dear, all this over again—examinations, worry, you've got this, you've got that." However, Francis insisted on having oxygen, so we went to see the doctor, a very cheerful, splendid man, Jean Mattei. He was most tactful. "Oh yes, fine," he said, "I'll lend you the apparatus, don't worry. My assistant will carry the cylinder to your room and I hope you'll be all right. Goodbye."

That night—I don't know whether it was another crisis or what—Francis said he was dying. I dragged the cylinder around the bedroom and to the bathroom, wherever he was, and still he was gasping for breath. In the morning I said we couldn't go on like that, I couldn't nurse him in the hotel and he must have this doctor come to see him. Mattei didn't come at the time he'd said. It got on to lunchtime and I said to the concierge, "Let me know the minute the doctor comes, won't you?" and went and had a brandy. I really felt a bit depleted by this time. When I was having lunch they announced the doctor had arrived, and by then I thought Francis would be carted off to hospital in an oxygen tent or something. But not a bit of it. "Madame, ce n'est rien, rien, rien," the doctor said. "There's nothing serious the matter with your husband, you'll see. He'll be fine, do not worry." He gave him vitamin injections, and pills, treating him for asthma and emphysema. Within three days Francis was up and about. I think that what this cheerful doctor really did was to restore his confidence. We argue about this, but as I see it Jean Mattei brought my husband a great surge of vitality and hope, and we've always been the most tremendous friends ever since.

I believe myself that life is a long road and that you're helped along it by different people. If you are lucky enough and courageous enough to stick to the middle of this road and not be sidetracked, then help will come. To me Vence was almost like the end of a pilgrimage; I went into the Church there and thanked God in a big way for bringing us to this final place of ours. I felt that this recovery was very miraculous. Throughout I was controlled and directed by a power outside myself. I felt that these were holy matters and must be kept private, but this was not to be.

78

8

I REMEMBER that when I was reluctant to leave the quiet of the country and come back with Giles to London, my friend Dr. Cyril Pink said, "What you are looking for is security and you can only find that in yourself. You must go back to London and try to see the interest of your life there. Even if it is difficult it is bound to be interesting." And how prophetic his words were.

By nature I am more of an artist than a business woman, and at that time I had no training whatever to make me a useful active director of Francis Chichester Limited, the Map and Guide business my husband had started up in 1945. At first he had worked on his own in one room, then gradually he had got a small staff together. I had never had much to do with maps, but I could see that some of the things he had invented (his famous Pocket Map, for instance) were far too good not to be looked after and promoted. So with the help of Geraldine Hill, a very bright public relations consultant who taught me all I know about P.R., we arranged for one or two window displays, for press information and so on. I found it all very exciting and was grateful for her generosity, as indeed I am still. But when Francis's health deteriorated, he seemed to lose interest in the business, and when he went into hospital, I knew this was another problem I must tackle. Just worrying what was going to become of this project wouldn't do the family fortunes any good.

Francis suggested that I should go to a Directors' Exhibition being held at the time, so I went down with a friend of mine, Tiny Burton, who has been personal assistant to many famous men. I was very fascinated by one of those telephones you carry in your pocket and asked if we could try one out. Now, of course, they are quite commonly used in hospitals and elsewhere, but it was a very new idea then and we were thrilled to hear the buzzer buzzing in my escort's breast pocket. I also noticed a Tack Stand and the courses in salesmanship they were offering;

I made up my mind to have a go at one of these. One very cold, grey morning I presented myself at the Tack Institute in Victoria, and I think I'm right in saying I was the first woman who had taken a course like this. There were thirty-one salesmen there. When we had to stand up and say who we were, I said I was Managing Director of Francis Chichester Limited, thinking that, after all, I was running the company and was a director. To my great joy, I found that nearly all the men in the room had already got my husband's map in their pocket. During the two or three days which followed, I was absolutely gripped by the instruction and advice we were given. I found that most of what we were doing in the business was good—Francis, of course, is very original and modern in his ideas—but that on the practical sales side there was more we could do. I learned a bit about mail order, for example, and although some of the things we were told about conducting correspondence and so on were things I had known all my life, I was impressed by the standard of the course and their general Christian approach to what counted in being a good businessman—or woman.

Back I came with great ideas on sales promotion, and soon I managed to get a display of our maps and guides in a shop down the road from the house. I highlighted the fact that, since Francis is a famous navigator, the maps must be good. Quite an obvious claim, but no-one seemed to have thought of putting it forward before. There were, of course, some awful experiences to cope with, as on the day when one of the girls came to me and said there was a director of the Savoy Hotel group on the telephone, very angry indeed and wanting all their hotels taken out of our Guides. So I thought to myself, "I must go and see this man." He turned out to be Mr. John Hannay, now Vice-Chairman of the Savoy Group, and he was very nice to me even though he pointed out some shattering mistakes which had got into print for lack of Francis's direct supervision. I promised all would be put right.

At this time our business had the most appalling overdraft and money was very tight. We seemed to be in debt to everybody and it was all a pretty good struggle. Yet despite my anxiety over Francis's illness, I did manage to get new ideas and find myself taking to this new responsibility. The thing that interested me most was the rhythm of business and the facts and figures.

Sheila and Francis on their wedding day, 25th February, 1937.

Sheila and her son Giles in the garden of The Fishing Cottage, Stitchcombe.

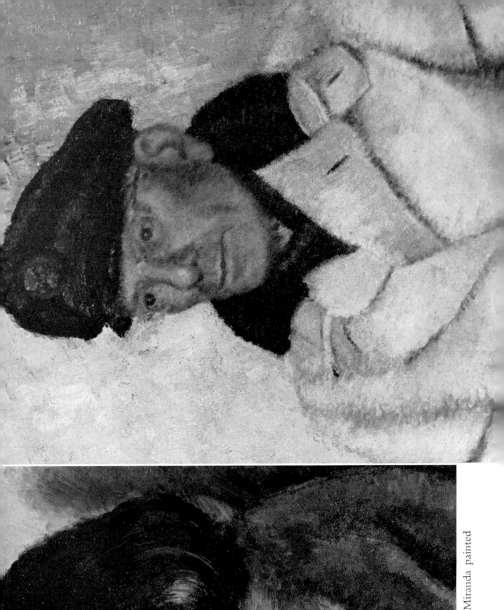
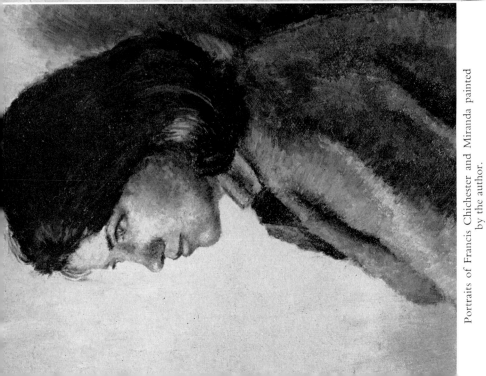

Portraits of Francis Chichester and Miranda painted by the author.

Throughout this time when I was trying to cope, I used to think of my millionaire grandfather and say to myself, "He was a good businessman; let's hope I've got some of it in me." I visited the works where the Maps and Guides were printed and bound. One of the things I learnt was the importance of giving compositors properly prepared typescripts to work from and what a difference this could make in time, trouble and expense. During this time, Monica Cooper, one of our Directors, gave me all her help and loyalty and has done so ever since. She started as my husband's secretary and has been with the company nearly twenty years. If Francis and I are both away, she takes charge of the business and looks after all our interests in a very competent way.

About this time I decided to compile my own guide. It was called *Sheila Chichester's Shopping and Fashion Guide*, but now the name has been changed to *London Woman*. My friend Joy Matthews, a very good journalist, wrote the text of the first edition for me. So many friends coming up to town had asked me where to shop and where to eat and so on that it seemed quite an idea to provide the answers in a small book women could carry around with them. I kept it personal and was adamant that there must be no advertising in it. A charming American banker said to me, "You're a brave girl but if you do a thing like that without advertisements, you're bound to run to ruin." Yet *London Woman* still goes on. Francis liked it so much that he's done one of his own called *London Man* and outsells me by ten to one, which isn't surprising since there are many more men than women in business wanting this kind of information. The maps in *London Woman* were, of course, my husband's, and they are absolutely first-class.

The aspect of the business which I personally found the most difficult was the production side and costing. These need good mathematical knowledge and specialised training, and you have to be very strong and tough, always getting after people on the telephone and insisting on things being done to schedule. We now have an excellent young woman, Thelma Rolfe, as our Production Manager and she copes ably with all these things. The planning side I'm interested in, but one has got to have very good judgment—public taste changes quickly—plus a capacity for very hard work and endurance. One of the ideas I had for my husband was to make a very big wall map of inner London, on a 14 inches to 1 mile scale. This was inspired by a visit to Paris where I saw a wonderful map of the French capital made by Blondel Larougerie. I picked things up as I went along, doing the best I could, and all this business was ticking over while Francis gradually recovered his strength. And the time was to come when he'd embark on three big Atlantic ventures and the world voyage, and as Vice-Chairman it fell to me to take full charge and responsibility while he was away, leaving everything running smoothly when I went to join him. Undoubtedly his sailing exploits have helped the business greatly, giving our customers confidence that they have got one of the finest navigators in the world designing their maps for them.

After my return to London from Wiltshire I had two great interests which weren't, like the business, thrust on me by circumstances, but much more a matter of following my natural bent. The first was painting and the second was learning more about psychology and healing. Though creative art was to be crowded out of my life once more, I have missed this and regret, too, that it has not been possible to be more in the company of genuinely artistic people, which is something I greatly enjoy. I hope soon to begin painting again, above all, portraits of people I think beautiful, rather saintly people, priests and other healers. One friend in particular, a physiotherapist, I'd very much like to do. I began to attend classes in painting at the end of the war, with Miss Sonia Mervyn, a brilliant teacher, but then my creative abilities turned in another direction. I had a child but I stopped painting. Now, one day a week, I began again, going to a class which Miss Mervyn ran for adult people like myself and some young ones who wanted to learn to paint in oils. I am grateful to her, among other things, for teaching me to keep my brushes clean and really look after my equipment. This may sound very simple, but one day I remember an art teacher saying to me, "I can't think why the children's work is so muddy looking." I said, "Let me look at their brushes." And it was obvious they just never cleaned them. I am certain any craftsman must look after his tools. Another thing she taught us was to use very good canvases, and in fact many of the class made their own up. I am afraid I was too lazy or too busy; I didn't do this. Though I was always dissatisfied with my work and terribly slow and convinced

I was the worst of these people, I remained fascinated by faces. It has always intrigued me that we all have a skull and the same features and so on, yet every single human being is different, with the occasional exception of identical twins. I used to try to catch the character of the sitters, and at home I took half my bedroom for painting. I did manage to do quite nice portraits of my husband and of my son, but there seemed less and less time, and with Francis's latest venture, the circumnavigation, this all got dropped again.

On the same day of the week as my painting class, I used to go to Harley Street in the evening and attend lectures at the Open Way. We were studying "What is Healing?" Dr. Cyril Pink and his wife Marguerite suggested my going along with them and used to pick me up in their car. At the same time I made friends with the Rev. Geoffrey Harding, now Executive Secretary of the Church's Council of Healing. After the lectures we drove Geoffrey to the station where he caught his train to the country. The object of Dr. Howe, who started this Group, was to encourage research into our experience of the common ground between psychiatry, the great religions and the modern scientific world view, in health and disease. We had some very interesting men and women from all walks of life to address us. They held different beliefs but there was no atheist among them.

One person we did have was the Maharishi who has since become famous for his connection with the Beatles. In those days he was a very quiet man—he probably still is. Other lecturers were Christmas Humphries, Dr. Woodard, different people whose talks fascinated me and gave me a great deal of help. I am intensely interested in personality and firmly believe there are diseases of personality which can be cured in various ways. Dr. Pink and Geoffrey Harding used to discuss and analyse the lectures for me as we drove to Paddington, for at first I used to find the psychotherapists in particular very abstruse. Occasionally I really didn't know what they were talking about, but at the end of a lecture on Dreams by a German doctor, I remember telling the lady sitting beside me that my head was bursting. "So is mine," she said. "He gave us enough for three or four lectures. The man crowded in far too much, and that is why you're feeling like that." She herself was a qualified pyschologist, so I found this very consoling.

83

Certainly I do not believe that any of us went there by chance. Without the wonderful experience of these sessions at the Open Way, I could not have come as I did through what was to follow, the prolonged crisis of my husband's illness. Dr. Pink, priest and doctor, has now died and I miss him very much indeed. He was a very holy person; in fact, I think, one of those quiet, unknown saints. When you went to him with a problem, he viewed it objectively, made you see it on a non-material, uncluttered level, and it seemed to fade away. With him I was always very conscious of the presence of God. Like Pope John, he had a strong charisma. He told me he felt it was necessary to be a priest as well as a doctor really to heal people, and this combination made him a very exceptional adviser.

Though I shall have more to say about prayer in connection with Francis's voyages, I should like to put here one thing I have learned about it: prayer is not asking but listening and giving. It is an output of power, and shared with others it becomes stronger. Two prayers which have always upheld me are these:

> All things are possible to him who believes,
> but they are less difficult to him who hopes,
> and still more easy to him who loves, and still
> more easy to him who perseveres in the practice
> of these three virtues.

Brother Laurence wrote this in 1666 in *The Practice in the Presence of God*. The other prayer is in St. Mark's Gospel, XI, verse 24:

> All things whatsoever ye pray and ask for, believe that
> ye have received them and ye shall have them.

I know it is easy enough to reel these things off, but to me they are something tested and infinitely helpful. When the Franciscan Brothers of Cerne Abbas intercede for a sick person, one of the Fathers told me, "We don't presume upon God to heal this person. That is His affair, but we hold him before God in our Minds, picturing him healed, and then we leave it to God."

I also believe in praying for others in the same group as the sick ones, and for the doctors and nurses who are caring for them.

9

B Y THE summer of 1959 Francis had built up his strength sufficiently to go as navigator in the big Italian yacht *Mait* on the Fastnet race and he thoroughly enjoyed this. When he came back it was time for us to go to Ireland to launch our new boat, *Gipsy Moth III*.

Before his illness developed to the dreadful extent it did, we had made a trip to John Tyrrell's yard at Arklow to see the boat. To my horror I found everything in the cabin was much too low. The berths seemed to be almost down to the ground, the sink and working-table were the old-fashioned kind where you had to bend your back, despite all our careful planning to have these at the right height. This wonderful boat which was going to be so comfortable, so much better than the old one! We spent a lot of time measuring up. It turned out that the water tanks had arrived too big and they had decided to bring the floor up rather than re-place them. Eventually we reached a compromise, and though the settees were always a bit low, the galley part and Francis's navigation table were all right.

That first visit to Ireland had been in chilly weather. I remember we stayed in the coldest pub I have ever been in. Francis and I shared a single bed and the blankets didn't really cover us. Such are the joys of being a yachts person! But this time it was one of those glorious heat waves that sometimes come at the beginning of September. I drove Francis, Giles and Martin Jones through the beautiful Irish countryside from Dublin in the most perfect weather; no crowds, no other cars, marvellous. When we rounded the corner and came down into Arklow, there was *Gipsy Moth* sitting up waiting to be launched. It was a great moment.

The following day there seemed to be some doubt about the time the tides would be suitable. I had hoped to have a blessing of the boat at the launch and had written to the rector of Arklow, but when I called at the vicarage I found he was away on holiday, so in fact it was Tubby Clayton who did this for us later on, in the Beaulieu River. That evening while we were having dinner someone came rushing up: "Quick, quick, the tides are right. Come at once!" So we flew down to the yard, I stood on a plank high in the air, and John Tyrrell said, "Be careful you don't step back when you christen her or you might fall off." I thought, "That might be it; better be careful." I named the boat *Gipsy Moth III*, dashed the champagne bottle on to her and broke it so well and truly that I got glass and champagne in my hair. She slid into the water.

The following day they went out for trials. I decided I would leave them on their own, and Giles and I found the most entrancing bay I've ever seen, miles of silver sand and blazing sunshine, and practically no-one there at all. We had some marvellous bathing and thoroughly enjoyed ourselves. As we drove back in the evening we saw *Gipsy Moth* sailing in the bay, looking very lovely with her white sails and her black hull. But she had a curious rocking movement which she always kept. It seems to be characteristic of many English boats, and in view of what she accomplished it didn't make much difference to her. During the rest of the week we hectically fitted out, bought stores and other necessities, had some hooks put up and so on, and on the Saturday we sailed in beautiful weather. Francis talked of going to the Scilly Islands but I put him off this. The helm was so stiff I felt a bit jittery, and I really thought the rudder would break, it was so difficult to move at all. The weather continued fine, very little wind, a certain amount of fog, and we proceeded slowly and finally reached the Helford River in Cornwall. We were glad to get in there and pick up a buoy. The Customs man came out and we all rowed ashore. Never have I seen a more lovely river.

We spent a few blissful days there, bathing and lolling about, decided the rudder wasn't too bad, and got her back to Beaulieu River after a very slow and peaceful sail. I enjoyed it but Francis was impatient because there was so little wind. This was a very fine autumn. In October we had a marvellous sail over to France with two great friends, Marston Tickell and Mike Richey, both famous navigators. The helm continued to be extremely tough. I could hardly push it over, and later in the autumn, when the boat was laid up, it was found that the strap didn't fit properly.

The start of the great Solo Trans-Atlantic Race came about

as far as I was concerned one day late in the autumn of 1959. I walked into my husband's office and found a fair-haired man he introduced to me as "Blondie" Hasler, the famous Cockleshell Hero Marine. They were discussing the idea of this race. Blondie turned to me and said, so naturally, "The idea is to cut down the chores in sailing." I immediately fell in love with this and thoroughly understood it. I've always thought there were far too many chores in sailing. I don't mean below—that is pretty simple because it is all so small. No, I mean on deck where in the past they had those terribly heavy warps and sheets, stiff canvas sails and ghastly great boathooks and so on. One of the most valuable things the Solo Race did for sailing was to advance a lot of very necessary ideas which have been a help to crews, ocean racers, and in fact all sailing people. Above all, of course, the wind vane; this self-steering device really developed from the race. There had been a few before, but nothing like the number now in use. And this is of immense benefit for women. One can often take a watch quite easily, but it's very tiring to take the helm for hours on end. With a Miranda—a wind vane such as we had, designed by Francis—there's no problem. It frees a man once for all to go sailing with his wife or girl-friend, needing no other crew.

This Trans-Atlantic Race was to be single-handed, the first of its kind, and I was fascinated to think of the entrants starting from the same port at the same time for the same destination, testing themselves and their boats against the loneliness of the ocean. I saw immediately that this would be the cure, the final cure, for my husband, that he needed this kind of venture; and so I encouraged Blondie and Francis in every way I could and very much enjoyed helping them. At this time I think Blondie had been trying for three years to get the race on its feet: it was considered rather dangerous and eccentric and people were nervous of it. The *Observer* had offered a prize of a thousand pounds but didn't make this public. The Slocum Society had turned down the project and so had one or two of the yacht clubs at Cowes. Francis said, "Why not try the Royal Western at Plymouth?" When they were in two minds about taking it, Francis, Blondie and Lindley Abbatt, representing the *Observer*, went down to Plymouth and talked to them. All was well in the end, largely due to Colonel Jack Odling-Smee, the Vice-Commodore at that time, and the *Observer* came into the open, offering a trophy instead of a cash prize. They did, however, pay each of the four contestants for the option on his story, and this was to be made up to a thousand pounds for the winner. After the Royal Western had agreed to start the race, the Slocum Society said they would finish it, and it was decided that Ambrose Light vessel in the approaches to New York Harbour would be the right place for the finish. Thinking of the Trans-Atlantic Race as it is today, and the number of entrants from all over the world in 1968, it is interesting to look back at the outset of it all with this project of the *Observer's* only eight years ago. The great international races which have grown out of it have been of immense benefit to yachting generally, both in gear and equipment, and recently the *Sunday Times* offered a five thousand pound prize for a non-stop voyage round the world.

Blondie was with us in our drawing-room one day when he suddenly said, "I want you to draw the sail numbers for this race, Sheila." At this time there were four entrants: Blondie and Francis, Dr. David Lewis (I found him a fascinating character. One of his interests in the race was to study the effects of solitude, and this intrigued me), and Valentine Howells, tall, handsome, bearded, also a glamorous and romantic figure. Later there was to be a fifth contestant, the Frenchman Jean Lacombe in his tiny *Cap Horn*. I was rather reluctant about drawing the numbers for the race because of Francis being in it, but Blondie had his way. He shook up the four numbers in Francis's old sailing fore-and-aft hat, and I drew number 1 for Francis. Whether this was fate or not, it was certainly curious, for he did win in the end, though everyone thought then that his boat was too big to be handled by one man.

This first race had a glamour about it which will never come again. Among the interesting acquaintances I made at the time was Lindley Abbatt, doing the promotion of the race for the *Observer*. Although he didn't know much about sailing, he could see the immense potential of the thing, as I did, and we used to telephone each other a lot to talk about it. And I hammered away trying to make the race well known and get general interest for it.

Some time early in 1960, February I think it was, I asked Francis if he could give me his estimated time of arrival in America. I was determined to show my faith in the race and wanted to book a passage on a boat arriving a few days before he expected to make it in *Gipsy Moth*. Francis said he believed it could be done in twenty-eight days, so I booked then and there on the *Flandres*, due in New York on July 5. I wanted to go on a French boat—I am very fond of French people and French food.

Interest in the race gradually mounted; by late Spring there were many enquiries and the Press began to get warmed up about it. We had great fun getting *Gipsy Moth* ready at Bucklers Hard, and at the beginning of June Francis and I sailed alone down to Plymouth where the other three contestants were waiting for us. Some radio/telephones had been lent them from America. People expected an awful lot of these, but Francis was the only one who got his messages through. He sent me two very important ones when I was waiting for him in New York. This was my first introduction to radio/telephones and prepared me for what was going to happen later on when Francis got the long range Kestrel.

The *Observer* gave a wonderful last-minute party on the night of June 10. About fifty or sixty people attended—and the fifth contestant who arrived, Jean Lacombe, was so tired that he fell asleep at the dinner. On the morning of June 11, four yachts started, *Cap Horn* following later because Jean was not ready. It was rough, there was a strong wind blowing, and Francis disappeared going very fast. That evening Dr. Lewis and *Cardinal Virtue* came back having been dismasted, but to David's eternal credit and seamanship the boat was repaired and he completed the race, coming in third.

Lloyds had been asked to report if they received any sightings of the yachts, which all carried their names in big letters, but they disappeared off into the blue in this rough weather. Later we had a gale off Land's End. People asked me if I wasn't nervous, but I didn't feel so in the least. I was thrilled with the whole thing and confident in the ability of these men to achieve what they had set out to do. After they had left, I planned to go back to London and stay in the office looking after our business. On the eve of my departure I gave a dinner party, asking all the ladies to wear trousers. I have always liked them and was taking several pairs with me to America, so I thought it would be rather fun to wear them on this occasion.

Going to America was a terrific adventure for me; I didn't

know anyone there, I was very short of money, I was leaving Giles behind, and one way and another felt I was taking a bit of a plunge. Before I left on June 28, we had received some positions for Val Howells in Eire, but otherwise we had heard nothing. When I took the train down to Plymouth, Francis's New Zealand partner came to see me off. He wasn't very cheering. "I can't understand your going like this when you haven't heard anything from Francis and they're not in," he said. "Why don't you wait?" However, he took me in the bar, we had a Dry Martini, and I set forth. My seat number was thirteen which has always followed me as a very lucky number. I laughed to myself when I saw this. Later on, my landing number was thirteen and I waited thirteen days for Francis from the date of his E.T.A.

I had taken an inside cabin on the *Flandres* because I couldn't afford anything better; it was a bit stuffy, but there it was. I started reading my cutting book about the race and discovered that the Lord Mayor of Plymouth had sent a letter of goodwill with each of the contestants to the Mayor of New York, which was something no-one had told me about in the rush of departure. The carrying of this message helped me to get the interest of our Consulate in New York City. After two days at sea, to my great joy and excitement I had a cable giving me Francis's position; *Gipsy Moth* had been sighted by *Mauritania*. I rushed up to the Captain and asked if I could see Francis's position on the chart and the track of *Flandres*. We, of course, were doing 500 miles a day, *Gipsy Moth* about 100, but I realised we might pass very close to her. I showed my cutting book to the Captain who up till then, like other people abroad, had thought me a crazy English-woman. He asked if my husband had a radio and said he would try and call him. "If we can find him," he said, "We'll alter course and have a look at him." I thought this extremely sporting of him, but when I went to bed that night, I heard the fog horns going and realised this put an end to our chance of seeing *Gipsy Moth*. The *Flandres* did try to signal Francis, but he was not listening, his station was not open at the time. A yacht cannot possibly man a radio all the time as they can do on a liner, so the Captain sent me a message to say he was very sorry but he wasn't able to contact Francis. Later on when Francis came in, I compared his track with the track of the *Flandres* and discovered we were only 15 miles S.S.E. of *Gipsy Moth III* at 5 p.m. on Friday, July 1.

We went on our way, and people on the ship started betting a bit on the race because by that time I'd had a cable from Chris Brasher to tell me that Blondie in *Jester* had been spotted north of Francis. It looked as though, if he did get a big wind, he might come down and cut in ahead of *Gipsy Moth*. The Captain's opinion was that Blondie was too far north and would have trouble getting down, which is in fact what did happen. He came in second, a week after Francis.

It was very hot when I arrived in New York on July 5. John Phlieger, Commodore of the Slocum Society, kindly met me and introduced me to some of his friends. One of them was Mariel Bonhame, a charming woman; the *Cap Horn*, which Jean Lacombe was sailing in the race, was one of her husband's yachts. Knowing my interest in healing, she took me to a service of healing at the wonderful church of the Heavenly Rest in New York City. I was deeply impressed with this. I also used to go to the Church of St. Bartholomew, which was almost next door to my hotel, the Sheraton East in Fifth Avenue. The church warden and his son were both yachtsmen and were very friendly to me. It was a time of waiting and of rumours; the American Press weren't very interested, but the coastguards were watching out.

Then a cable came from Francis. He'd sent it when he was just south of Cape Race on July 8: "Please tell my wife regret I've been delayed." He had a job to get his radio/telephone to work, but he had got the message through on the day he had said he would arrive in New York. This caused great excitement, and I was thrilled to be able to take it to an old friend of ours, a famous navigator, Alf Loomis, and tell him Francis's position. "He won't be in before July 21," he said. I thought he was being pessimistic, but of course he knew the Eastern seaboard frightfully well; it is a slow bit, where you get fogs and calms, and he was spot on. On July 13 I had another cable. By now the English Press were full of interest and started ringing me up. On the morning of July 17, Ed Connolly of the *Daily Sketch*, who'd interviewed us at Plymouth, telephoned me from London and said, "Francis has got the race in the bag. I've just been speaking to the U.S. coastguards and he was seen off Nantucket on Saturday. He'll be in tomorrow."

I talked on the phone to one of the coastguards. On his forecast I decided I would try to hire a boat and go out to Ambrose Light vessel to meet Francis. The day before, Teddy Robbins (the yachtsman who had sailed with us in *Figaro* in 1957) came to New York with his wife to see me and look after me, and he advised me where to find a boat. We engaged a fishing boat called the *Edith G* and she sailed from Sheep's Head Bay. Some of the members of the Press who were interested in Francis came with me. We had a very nice outing but he didn't turn up. That evening Chris Brasher, who'd been sent out by the *Observer*, arrived, and we also had news of *Jester*, sighted by the *Queen Mary*. We began to wonder if Blondie was going to come in first. Next day, with Chris Brasher and other representatives of the Press I went out again in *Edith G*, but again it was an abortive trip. It's very curious how rumours go round and are picked up and accepted. In my more recent experience this has happened even with all the careful positions we've had. Anyway I said, "I'm not going out again until I've got more information."

It was an embarrassing and a frustrating time. I have never known so many phone calls; messages were pushed under the door, and wherever I went the Press were there. I could see they were on the verge of starting a panic story, headline "Missing Yachtsman", but I put my foot down firmly on this and kept saying Francis would probably be in the next day. And I kept going down to the hairdresser, and when they asked what I was doing, I said I was getting ready to go and meet my husband. The afternoon before he actually arrived I went to the cinema; it was nice and quiet in there and I enjoyed that. When I got back to the hotel they were all round me again. Chris Brasher had gone out in a plane to try to spot Francis. However, I went to bed and slept very well, though I remember that I woke in the night, looked at my chart again and thought, "How could he be in? He can't be in before tomorrow from where he is." I'd been rushed by all these people.

At eight in the morning of July 21 the telephone rang. "It's eureka, it's eureka! We found him, we found him." This was Chris. He and Malcolm Douglas Hamilton went out in a plane, but I went out in *Edith G* for the third time, accompanied by Captain Jim Percy, who had come to greet Francis as Warden of the Guild of Air Pilots and Navigators. Members of the Press and photographers were also on board. We arrived at Ambrose Light vessel, again we waited and no sign of him. Suddenly we picked up his voice, Francis's voice, on the radio telephone. This was a terrific moment. He gave his course to Captain Percy, we shot across, and within twenty minutes we saw a white sail appear above the horizon. Everybody asked me, "Is that your boat?", and I looked very carefully, not wishing to make any mistake after all these rumours he was arriving, missing and so on. But I clearly saw Miranda, the wind vane, sticking out like a white bustle, and I knew this was my husband. We saw him and waved, he waved back. He had still a little way to go before passing Ambrose Light vessel. The Press wanted me to draw alongside and greet him, but having taken part in ocean races myself, I said, "You can't do that. He'd be disqualified." Another Press boat arrived and the excitement was terrific, people getting quite violent and rushing off in a faster launch to take photographs to get off to their papers.

We all went along to watch him pass the Ambrose Light vessel to win the race. I felt a wonderful exhilaration and remember thinking how great a thing it is to have faith and to cast your bread on the waters. This had been proved to me: Francis had made the grade, and above all, of course, I realised this would put his illness behind him. I was more pleased about that, even then, than I was about his winning the race.

Finally he tied up. His cabin was a pretty good shambles, he'd had some very rough weather and he didn't seem to have any lights, but we had a candle and drank the champagne I'd brought with me from England for the winner. When we got ashore, Mariel Bonhame seemed to appear from nowhere with her car, and after a call at the Sheep's Head Bay Yacht Club, where they were most welcoming—Americans are wonderful to you when you've achieved something—she drove us back to my hotel. Chris Brasher had ordered a lovely supper for us, with bottles of wine and I don't know what, but he says we both fell asleep in the middle and he took the meal out and left us lying on our beds. Next morning we woke up early, both feeling on top of the world. Chris Brasher in his pyjamas was telephoning the story to the *Observer*, who'd kept a big space for it, and there was a Press Conference, with the British correspondents terribly interested and the Americans not very. Our Press people decided this was because Americans like togetherness and we like alone—with it all. Later the British Consul-General took us to City Hall to deliver the letter the Lord Mayor of Plymouth had sent to the Mayor of New York, who not only gave us a book to take back as a present to Plymouth but also a gift for ourselves with the inscription: "You and your wife are ever welcome in the City of New York." I thought this delightful.

Then came a period of exciting hospitality from an American cousin, Mrs. Dick du Pont, who had been a Chichester. She kept ringing up and asking when we would visit her at Cape Cod. Eventually she asked her son Felix to fetch us in his private plane, a Comanche. As in my first trip in Francis's little plane, I was rather nervous. We seemed to fly in and out of the skyscrapers of New York City. We zoomed over City Island where *Gipsy Moth* was lying and down Long Island Sound, over Newport—such enormous houses—and finally arrived at Hyannis Airport. We drove to Indian Point, a short distance away, where Cousin Dick has a lovely estate on Oyster Harbours. Felix's wife Marka was there, which started a friendship that has gone on ever since.

They gave us a wonderful welcome, and in the evening there was a dinner given for us. In spite of the heat, Francis put on his green velvet dinner jacket which had sailed with him, and this pleased them very much. Laurence Hamilton, a grandson of Pierpont Morgan, who once had the biggest steam yacht in the world, said a wonderful Grace, which he ended: "Thank God for bringing this great yachtsman to our table tonight." There is something very marvellous about Americans and their dignity and warmth. After some splendid days here, bathing and sunbathing, coping with Press calls and finishing off articles, we had to tear ourselves away and return to the burning heat of New York. We had planned to sail back to England together in *Gipsy Moth* by way of the Azores, and time was running out. I was beginning to fuss a bit about Giles, who had been left behind and had just had his fourteenth birthday. He had spent the summer holidays with friends and would soon be going back to Westminster.

The boat had to be fitted out and fresh stores put on, all of which seemed to me a big chore in those days. We managed to pack up at the Sheraton East Hotel and get aboard. Lying in City Island in this blazing heat was very trying; we had no air conditioning, no ice box, no awning. But somehow we managed to survive, and during this time when we were waiting to sail we were proud to fly the special flag of the City of New York, which was presented to the four singlehanders.

Sailing back to England for me was a big adventure. I had never done a long ocean passage alone with Francis. Racing and cruising in European waters and round the coast of Britain, yes, but this was something different again: a 3,800 mile passage with a stop at Horta on Fayal in the Azores. Marka and Felix du Pont came to see us off. We said goodbye with great regret to them and the many other friends we'd made during our visit to America.

On August 24 we left at ten-thirty in the morning. I certainly wouldn't have attempted this voyage without the wind vane, which is like a second helmsman. I was very lucky in this passage as far as the Azores because we really had very good weather. It is unusual to get winds here beyond Force 7, but most of the way we had glorious sunshine and beautiful blue seas. It was a lovely lazy, happy existence. Miranda took the helm for us so that there was not much work to be done, and the nights were really wonderful. I used to go and sit in the cockpit with the moon shining brightly and all the stars out, the sails just billowing out and the ship sighing as she went on her way. This sort of weather went on for days and Francis became somewhat frustrated. I enjoyed watching the dolphins playing round the bow; I also saw a shark which was the colour of brandy, accompanied by his pilot fish. We saw a few steamers but on the whole seemed to have the ocean to ourselves.

After a while we started having more varied weather. There were squalls and heavy rolling. The Gulf Stream is like a river flowing in the ocean and you get wind against tide conditions which can make it very bumpy and uncomfortable. On September 9 I had the worst fright of the whole voyage. We were nearly run down by a steamer called *Alcoa Pointer*. When you are in a small yacht, to see an enormous bow towering above you is something not easily forgotten. They called out, "Where are you for?" I answered, "Horta," and thought he had finished with us. But the ship came back and an American officer appeared. "I hear you are out of water." I called back, "NO. We are going to Horta." He put up an American flag, we put up the Blue Ensign and we both went on our way. These were leisurely, delightful days; I used to lie on my bunk reading and meditating; beyond worrying about how Giles was and feeling out of touch with him I didn't have a care in the world.

As we got nearer the Azores the weather did become a little rougher, but looking back on what I was in after we left Horta on the last leg of the passage, this really wasn't bad at all and only seemed so to me because it was my first long voyage. On the seventeenth we celebrated Francis's birthday with a bottle of wine. A great excitement two days later, when we sighted Pico in the early morning. Francis called me up, and there it was, surrounded by cloud. It was too rough to get in to Horta that night, so we hove to and next day battled in; it was a Force 8 gale into the Channel, the tide with us but the wind against. We made port at four in the afternoon escorted by some delightful Portuguese who came out to meet us in a launch.

I fell in love with Horta and the island of Fayal and the people who lived there. Their warm friendship and courtesy reminded me of happy days spent in Portugal long ago. Particularly I was grateful to John Farria and his charming wife Claudine, and also Peter and his father at the Café Bleu. But it was getting late—the chill of autumn was already in the air—and I felt now that I wanted to get home, and above all see Giles again. I looked longingly at one or two steamers which came in and thought that, after all, it wouldn't be letting Francis down to go back in one of these, but then again I felt I wanted to complete the passage with him. We stayed ten days, delayed by waiting for a parcel from England that Francis wanted and which had been held up by rough weather. There were also repairs to be done to the petrol tank and one or two other items, apart from the fresh stores to be loaded on.

The weather became progressively worse, and I felt a bit apprehensive when we set sail again on the morning of October 3. Our friends John Farria and Peter came with us and escorted us by the pilot launch. I was very sad to say goodbye to them and look forward to the day when we can all meet again. Horta to me was a little haven of peace and happiness in the middle of the Atlantic Ocean, a sharp contrast to the rush and bustle of New York City.

My apprehensive feelings were justified, for within five and a half hours we were hove to under bare poles, with huge seas

Meeting Francis off Ambrose Light vessel winning first Single-Handed Trans-Atlantic Race.

Sheila with Francis, Blondie Hasler, David Lewis, Valentine Howells (the original single-handers) and Ritchie Symons a press officer, before the first Single-Handed Race, 1960.

Sheila at the tiller of *Gipsy Moth III* sailing under Brooklyn Bridge at the start of her voyage across the Atlantic, August 1960.

Being presented with a bouquet by Sir Max Aitken at a party to celebrate Francis's election as "Yachtsman of the Year".

near Sao Jorge. This is a sinister looking island, very dark and rising sheer out of the sea. I must say I was scared, and I don't think Francis liked it either. However, he cooked a hearty lunch of eggs and fried potatoes while I took the helm, feeling I was going to be pulled into the sea at any moment, we were rolling so heavily. But we managed to clear the Island safely by night. It was blowing Force 9 and next morning it was still very rough. There were huge seas running, like black mountain ranges. Waves were crashing on the boat; they were about twenty feet high, I'd say, with foaming tops. This rough weather continued day after day. When it stopped for a while and we had peace, I almost missed the screaming wind, all was so quiet. And one felt that more was to come. Another storm came up, the barometer went on falling, which always fills me with dread. But *Gipsy Moth III* was a remarkably steady boat, particularly if you put up a storm jib and trysail.

One of my fears in very rough weather was at night when Francis had to go on the foredeck to change sail. The noise of the seas and winds were so great that I couldn't hear another thing, so I asked him just to carry a torch so that I could see this flashing about. Had he gone overboard I doubt if I could have saved him. But I got used to this, like everything else, and would lie quietly in my bunk until he came down again. I didn't really fancy going out on wild nights and standing in the cockpit worrying about him.

As we got nearer to English waters it became much cooler and got dark early. We lit our stove, had one or two quiet autumn days with reasonable seas, and on one occasion a great big basking shark came right alongside us. It was certainly as long as *Gipsy Moth*. Off Ushant we saw a huge liner all lit up one evening. I pictured the people going down dressed for dinner and wondered what it would feel like. At this time we suddenly picked up the B.B.C. and heard the chimes of Big Ben. Although in some ways I was pleased to hear these sounds, I was sad too, because on an ocean passage you live in a little world of your own, and in spite of worries over rough seas, it is very peaceful and restorative mentally and physically.

On Sunday, October 16, in the afternoon, Francis suddenly said to me, "You ought to be able to see the Lizard Light now." I looked, and there to my great thrill was a light looming. After fourteen days at sea, to see a light like this is very exciting and I can well understand how navigators love their work. I was hoping to have a nice quiet sail to Plymouth, but it was not to be. The weather became rough again, and as we were going into Plymouth it was blowing about Force 8. We got into Millbay and were trying to tie up; I was on the helm, but our motor had no reverse to it, a fetish of the designer's. Francis was up forward. A man high up on the wharf threw me a warp and called out, "Hard Hard astern, Miss", and I called out, "I can't." It is an unpleasant feeling if you cannot stop, but if your engine won't reverse there is nothing you can do about it. However, the warp stopped us. Five minutes later the B.B.C. arrived. "Do go out and put your sails up again. We didn't have a chance to get a picture of you coming in," they said. But I'm afraid we didn't feel like putting up our sails again. We were in port and glad to be there.

This was the beginning of our friendship with David Smeaton; he interviewed us then and we have been friends ever since. After an ocean passage one is very natural ashore, as one is meant to be, because the sea simplifies you, makes you aware of living. You become optimistic and enthusiastic and life seems to be very uncomplicated. I only wish this feeling lasted but unfortunately it doesn't.

After a while George Everett, secretary of the Royal Western, came along to see us. We were delighted to see him, and he seemed pleased also that we were safely in. He complimented us on the state of our yacht, which as a woman pleased me very much. I think it is important to keep your boat fresh and clean on a long voyage; however rough the weather, there is usually time to tidy up before you come into port.

Looking back on the passage, and Francis agrees with me here, it was one of the most wonderful things we've done together in our married life. In the good weather we had to the Azores, we were able to spend hours in the cockpit, and those wonderful nights in the bright moonlight with the stars shining and the ship sailing along like some great ghostly bird are things I shall never forget. I was also glad to have been out in some rough weather and to have managed to get used to it; I felt a feeling of achievement and the completion of something I was proud to have done.

It was my sister Kathleen's birthday the day after we landed and I spoke to her on the telephone. I was never to see her again: she died very suddenly a week or two later. This was a great shock to me and a great grief. Until this happened, it was marvellous to be home, to have all the comforts of shore life, a hot bath, a comfortable bed, and eating and drinking on terra firma. I was overjoyed to get back to London and see my son again, and we really had a wonderful winter after that. Francis was made Yachtsman of the Year and life seemed very good.

No-one knows how to give a party better than the *Daily Express* and Max Aitken's Yachtsman of the Year parties are justly famous. I shall always remember how wonderful people were to us and what a wonderful evening that was. I don't think any of the things which have happened to us since were quite as exciting as that first time. Max presented me with a bouquet and said, "I am doing this because Sheila Chichester sailed home with her husband." Later that Spring of 1961, Prince Philip agreed to come and give away the prizes for the Solo Race. Seeing Francis receive his prize filled me with gladness.

10

DURING this time the business was struggling along. As usual, there were some staff problems to be solved when we got back. On the other hand, the publicity was helping sales, and we had Joy Weeks doing our production, a very competent woman who had also looked after Giles in our absence. The headmaster at Westminster had kept an eye on him too. When Giles was told his father had won the race, he said, "Oh, I know that." There was a radio in someone's study, and they had listened in to the news.

After we had paid our usual visit to the South of France, Francis told me he meant to try and do a record-breaking passage to America. He thought his time of forty days was very slow and believed it could be done in under thirty days. First of all he talked to John Anderson of the *Guardian*, who wrote about solo sailing in a very understanding way. Francis offered to sell the *Guardian* a daily radio story throughout the passage, and after discussions with the Editor in Manchester, this was accepted. Colonel Whitbread, who had always taken great interest in Francis's exploits in the air and at sea, and who is himself a very brilliant aviator and yachtsman, also agreed to help Francis.

So once more there were frantic preparations: the testing out of Marconi sets (Francis had to take his wireless operator's certificate, and got it), and the arrangement of daily reports from him on the radio/telephone to Brent radio terminal. Colonel Whitbread gave a wonderful dinner at Plymouth which the Lord Mayor attended. Tubby Clayton wrote a special Grace for it; we had speeches from John Anderson and a toast to the Lady (that was me) from Donald McCullough, originator of the B.B.C. Brains Trust, and then next day Francis sailed. He never failed with his daily reports, and I sincerely hope the *Guardian* benefited from their covering of this story because they had helped so much. Great credit must go to John Anderson and the Marine Department of the G.P.O. who pioneered it all.

Meeting Francis in New York was easy this time, knowing exactly where he was. The morning of my departure I had his position as usual, given me by the *Guardian* who had got it from Brent. This was my first jet flight and was an exciting experience for me, especially when we flew over *Gipsy Moth* off Nantucket. We were about 35,000 feet up, and it fascinated me that the yacht could be seen from a jet plane with the naked eye. Laurence Hamilton met me outside the Customs, and as soon as we got to the Sheraton East Hotel there was a press conference. Alistair Cook came, the first of those great journalists I had ever met. He had a jaunty straw hat and striped blazer.

Next afternoon Laurie asked me to get an overnight bag packed; he'd chartered a special yacht to meet Francis and would come to fetch me. *Shadow Isle* was very grand. We had a crew of four, a chef who had cooked for Adlai Stevenson, and Harold Manning, a professional skipper who takes command of the biggest yachts in American waters. He was very charming to me. "I usually work for millionaires," he said, "although I have a little boat of my own. I've never met anyone quite like you." "Why?" I asked. "Very few women would be prepared to stay on board in these conditions." We had tied up alongside Staten Island and there was really a very nasty swell. But I'm used to this in boats and was enjoying the comfort of this big yacht, although I was a bit tired.

To fill in the time waiting for Francis, Laurie suggested next day that we should cruise round Staten Island, the Quarantine Station. We got about halfway round and were cruising along very gently and enjoying the glorious sunshine when I looked at the smoke stacks and could see the wind had changed. "Laurie," I said, "Look at that smoke." "What of it?" he asked. "The wind has changed," I said, "Francis will be coming in quicker." With that he said, "My God, you're right." Captain Manning turned back all engines full power, and we thundered back to base.

After a lot of telephoning and agitation—Francis couldn't contact the American coastguards though he did in fact speak to the *Guardian* in London three minutes before he reached Ambrose Light vessel—we heard where *Gipsy Moth* was. Suddenly a man on a motor bike arrived and put a telegram in my hand. When I opened it I thought I was dreaming. It came from John F. Kennedy, a very delightful message of congratulation to

Francis. I decided to put this away and tell no-one for the moment, though I felt a bit guilty keeping it from Laurie. We went off down the river in such a hurry that Alistair Cooke only just got on board in time; the other journalist, Rex Herne from the *Guardian*, got left behind, and so did the camera man.

Over dinner, which we ate in great style, I felt I must tell Laurie about the telegram. When I produced it he was so excited I thought he was going to let it blow away. "I must tell the Press, I must tell the Press," he said. When I protested, he answered that they did public relations in a different way in America and rushed off. This worried me because I thought it was going against our luck.

During the excitement we nearly missed Francis by going to the wrong Light vessel. "Isn't that Scotland Light vessel we're going to?" I said to Laurie. "Oh, my dear, yes it is," he said, and we changed course for Ambrose Light vessel. Just as night was falling, Francis appeared, looking really wonderful. He always seems to bring his boats in looking shiny and neat and white sails well cared for, not at all the battered image that one could expect. And he laughs and says it's me, that he's afraid not to clean up before he comes in. But he didn't know I was on *Shadow Isle*, and while everyone was rushing and shouting and calling out to him, I retired to the back, sat down and thought, "Well, I'll just wait and enjoy it quietly on my own." Alistair Cooke came and joined me.

Then followed one of the most frightening and hectic trips I've ever seen for Francis. By this time it was pitch dark and it was 4th July, Independence Day, so there were masses of fireworks going up. Francis was sailing very fast, New York Harbour was crowded with shipping and long half-mile tows of barges in the middle which were unlit. One other launch appeared—I think it belonged to *Paris Match* or one of the French newspapers —and when finally Francis hove to and his petrol motor would not start after the Atlantic passage, this launch gave him a tow. Outlined against these terrific fireworks going up on Coney Island, the yacht looked like a great white moth, quite magnificent. In the end we all managed to tie up at Staten Island, and since there was to be a Press Conference in the morning, only one or two people came on board, including Alistair, of course, to get a dispatch off to the *Guardian*.

The thing that stands out in my mind about the next day's Conference was a reporter asking me at the end if he could read his script to me so that he could get it away quickly. When he'd finished, I said, "But you've missed the whole point of the story: the amazing communications, this instant reporting, daily, by the Kestrel set. On a tiny yacht, it's never been done before." "Oh," he said, "That was an *English* set, Ma'am." None of the other newspapers mentioned it either, and though we invited John Sibley of the New York *Times* to speak from *Gipsy Moth* to the *Guardian* offices in London, person to person, even then I don't believe he was really convinced but still half-thought we were picking up a land line in America. The telegram from President Kennedy was a highlight of interest, naturally. Francis was photographed receiving it, he sent back a suitable reply, and the pictures in the press of all this were very exciting.

We got under way for City Island, Francis and myself, the skipper of *Shadow Isle* and Laurence Hamilton, along with a Press boat with lots of television people. At the Statue of Liberty we were asked to heave to; there had been a message from the *Queen Elizabeth* that she was coming down the river and wanted to see us. They saluted us, we dipped flags to each other, and this was a great moment. Later on, some months later, we were sailing in the Solent when we met her, and the little ceremony was repeated. After *Gipsy Moth* was tied up, Laurie took us off on *Shadow Isle* to some quiet waters where we rested overnight. It's quite fantastic what practical thought the Americans take for one's comfort and the kindness and hospitality they show.

A few days later we set off on *Gipsy Moth* for one of the nicest cruises I have had in my life. Sailing in Long Island Sound really is a dream, and on the whole this was a quiet, informal trip, ending up at Cape Cod where all our du Pont relations came out and gave us a great welcome. *Gipsy Moth* was tied up at the end of their pier and was fitted out during the next few weeks, very happy ones with some fabulous beach parties and everyone being charming and encouraging.

This time we'd decided that Giles should come out and sail back with us. He was sixteen now, and though I had some misgivings, wondering whether I was right to take him, just as on my first transatlantic trip I'd worried whether it was right to leave him in England when something might happen to both

Francis and myself on the way back, it all turned out wonderfully. His school holidays began at the end of July, and he had to have a little time in America or he would never have forgiven us, so we eventually sailed on August 13. That morning Francis read me stories of wrecks on the shoals near Pollocks Rip just to encourage me. The boat seemed very overloaded and of course being three in the yacht meant much less room. To my horror the forecast was Easterly, which meant going straight on the wind. We had a wonderful send-off, however, starting at noon with an escort of friends in little yachts, power boats and small launches. All Giles's young friends from the Wiano Yacht Club came too, and I can still see the Commodore's son, aged eleven, in his little skip and remember how good he was about turning back when Francis said it was time to go home.

I think Francis had quite a hard passage with us, especially at the beginning when we both felt very seasick. We had a hectic night in Pollocks Rip and in the early morning of the fourteenth, when Francis felt he could relax because we had cleared the shoals, he asked me to take a watch. It was uncanny sitting there in thick fog and hearing fog horns all round us. Once in a while during this week we had sunshine, quiet seas and a gentle sail, but the night of August 18 was terrible, with a gale Force 8, heavy rolling and big seas running. A wave came into the cabin. Some of that passage was very disagreeable for me and I felt ghastly. My bunk was too short— no-one had had time to make it the right length— and I had to hold myself in day after day, in the very rough weather, which was exhausting. I'd been rather frightened Francis might get tough with Giles and send him out on the foredeck, but there I was quite wrong, for he was splendid with our son. And for five days we had wonderful sailing; from the twentieth to the twenty-fifth we had the sort of run sailors dream about and rarely get. It was still too rough to go in the cockpit much, but we made up some sleep and had a bathe in a heavy rain squall, which was refreshing. For the last twelve days I had got over my seasickness, and though we had more big seas and bumpy nights, we had perfect conditions at the very end. Giles, who had been very seasick on this passage, which seemed rather like riding a horse in a steeplechase for weeks on end, turned out to be an extremely good seaman.

At eleven o'clock on the night of September 8, Giles and I

suddenly saw three lights looming in an arc; Bishop Rock, Wolf Rock, and Lizard Light dead ahead. It was a brilliant starry night, we were reaching along very comfortably, lovely smooth water and the marvellous feeling that we'd made the grade and that it had been all worthwhile. I had never realised before how many ships come round Land's End and through the Western Approaches; there seemed to be thousands of them. We were going so fast that we had to heave to and hang about Eddystone a good while because we had made a date with the B.B.C. and the *Guardian*. However, in the end they met us at the breakwater and took films and pictures. We tied up at Plymouth at twelve-fifty on September 9 and a lot of journalists came aboard. Before we left America, we had been given an enormous cheese (until I went there I had no idea they produced cheese like this; I think it was specially treated with wine or something) and the press men enjoyed this very much. Next morning we were invited to visit the Lord Mayor of Plymouth and the Royal Western Yacht Club gave a delightful dinner for us.

That night at the Grand Hotel I was surprised to be visited by a *Daily Express* man who said his Editor particularly wanted an interview with me. When I finally agreed, partly, I suppose, because I thought this was something new, for the ladies not to be by-passed, he did a very good article for the middle page. So I was glad afterwards that I'd given this interview. One thing I said in it was that Giles and I both led such busy lives, I in the business and he of course at school, that we had very little time to talk to one another. On this passage we spent days and days together and were able to communicate; I found out a great deal more about what he was doing and feeling. This time on *Gipsy Moth*, the three of us together, living the natural, simplified life you lead at sea, was a great experience for all of us. Francis's record-breaking trip across the Atlantic and our return with him were now part of our family story.

Gipsy Moth III had her final big venture in the second Solo Trans-Atlantic Race in 1964. During the last two days of the race, when it became quite clear that Francis wasn't going to win it, that he would be beaten by Eric Tabarly, people suddenly got terribly British and kept saying, "I do wish he could win," and "Why didn't he have a new boat?" Francis's cousin Lord Dulverton rang me up and asked the same question, "Why didn't

Francis have a new boat to beat this Frenchman?" "Two reasons, Tony," I answered, "Time and money." So he said, "I will provide him with a suitable vehicle" (those were his exact words) "for the next race. I want you to tell him that and I want to come round and see you." So he came to St. James's Place and in a most sincere way offered this new boat to help Francis. So I said, "I will tell him."

After this I flew to America to meet Francis, who came in second, and again we had wonderful hospitality and a very happy visit to Newport and our du Pont cousins at Oyster Harbours. While we were trying to get *Gipsy Moth* ready to sail back across the Atlantic a third time, Giles joined us. My bunk had been lengthened, which I was glad of and quite sure this would make a great difference to my comfort on the passage. But very acute business problems had cropped up at home, and I felt I couldn't leave the staff to cope on their own. It seemed better just to fly back, so rather sadly I saw *Gipsy Moth* sail away, and returned by air to London. Though I was reluctant to decide this, I thought that, after all, it would be very nice for Francis and Giles to do this alone together.

While we were in America, I told Francis of Tony's offer of a new boat, and it wasn't long before he said to me, "I've got a project. I want to do a solo circumnavigation, at speed, round the world." He gave me his proposed plan to show the Press and find out whether a paper would take his story of this voyage. I was absolutely gripped by this plan; as I read it it brought a breath of fresh air to my mind. Back in London, we had a meeting with Tony, who insisted Francis must have the best boat possible and the best builder.

We had been in touch with John Illingworth some time before. He had sketched a boat which he called *New York Express*, intended for the second Solo Trans-Atlantic Race, but of course it wasn't built then because of the time and money problems. I think it's a great mistake to build a boat too quickly, as far too many are built; this can lead to disaster. I don't believe they had time to test Eric Tabarly's trimaran before the 1968 race, and he was very wise to turn back as he did. Anyway, we had a great many talks about design for Francis's new boat, and during this time we sold *Gipsy Moth III*. Giles and I were rather sad; we had become attached to her.

Francis has written fairly extensively about all the worry we had over the building of *Gipsy Moth IV*, so it will suffice to say I did my best to keep everybody co-ordinated and regretted very much that no-one agreed it would be a good idea to make notes at the meetings of these highly expert men, who gave their views and said they'd remember it all. Just a small amusing example was that after the Marconi Marine people and the overseas communications men of the Post Office had got together and were leaving, I said I'd like their telephone numbers. Francis said, "Really, fancy asking them for these!" and everybody laughed. But within a week he was asking me for their numbers and my note of them was very useful.

Hodders, our publishers, gave us a contract for the book on Francis's round the world voyage and offered us an advance in their usual generous fashion. Tony agreed to pay for the boat, which after many delays got under way. Francis wanted to leave towards the end of August 1966, and you would have thought that with planning and meetings at Gosport all through the winter of '64 and an actual start in building her made in May'65, there would have been time enough. But there wasn't. Everything seemed to be done in a hurry, and I don't think people realise how much there is to do and to order for a yacht, all the hundreds of life-and-death things they have to have. Everybody did their best, but this was a pioneering venture and there are not enough trained craftsmen in England today. Let's face it, a custom-built yacht is now a rare luxury.

In my own mind I liken yachts to the great Maisons de Couture where just a few dresses are made for a few individuals. Nowadays, of course, Marks and Spencer have shown what wonderful clothes can be produced by brilliant organisation and mass-production, and they have a very big public buying from them. As more and more people have yachts and there's a bigger market, everything will change; it will become possible then to put a price on a boat whereas now the costs seem to rise and rise and the cost turns out far higher than it was in the first contract. And the number of people sailing has already increased enormously. When I sailed in the Solent as a girl, there would be two or three yachts in Yarmouth; now you can hardly get in, there's a forest of masts. This is good, for I feel man has got to take to the sea, and I am all for the family sharing in any sailing projects as much as they can. At sea, you are either working hard or lying on your bunk or having the time and quiet to meditate or read. You feel you're really living, using your body and your mind, particularly if you're navigating and have the ever-changing scene to keep you on your toes; the sea and winds are always changing. I wouldn't have wanted to go on this circumnavigation; racing is too uncomfortable, but sailing for pleasure is a very different and wonderful thing.

The whole circumnavigation project was kept deadly secret. Francis kept saying to me, "I'm quite sure someone else will start out to do the same thing as soon as they know about this." It seemed to me extraordinary he should feel this way about such an ambitious plan. Yet I felt it was quite natural for Francis to do it and was only concerned that he should have help and support and a good boat. Above all, I was interested in the communications side of it, the twice-weekly messages he meant to send to the *Guardian*. "This project must be shared with other people to keep up their interest," he said all along. It's a great luxury for a yachtsman to be able to vanish off on a lone voyage, and the fact is that those people who do it are opting out of society; they have all the excitement and pleasure for themselves. Sponsorship, which has come under criticism lately, is a commitment; it takes time and is no sinecure if you regard it in a responsible way.

Summer holidays at Camper's yards held up building the boat so that it was autumn '65 before there seemed to be real progress. This was running it pretty fine, and that winter was a nightmare. We used to go down to Gosport every week, catching a train about eight in the morning and having interminable discussions in the boat; so many experts and everyone wanting something different. I remember one occasion when the designer of the mast fittings travelled with us on the return journey, planning the thing with Francis in a shaky B.R. Buffet car over a cup of tea, and then getting off in a great rush at Havant. "How can they get it right like this?" I thought. I was feeling very tired and exhausted, and when we managed to get off for our usual winter walking holiday in France, I was quite ill for a couple of days. But soon I was doing my ten miles a day to Francis's twenty—he starts off early and works off his energy circling all round the hills, I meet him, and we come back together. By then he's ready to walk home at a normal pace with me: just one example of how it is to live with a man of colossal energy who likes me to share things, which isn't always easy to work out.

We had arranged for a Press Conference on April 22 at our publishers. Meanwhile, just before Easter and my birthday, I had an accident to my eye. A heavy knob on a curtain cord hit it fair and square, and next morning I couldn't see properly. All the same I went down with Francis to help fit out the boat. When we got back it was obvious I must go to an oculist. He said I'd had a haemorrhage in that eye, and my own doctor ordered me a month's rest in bed to cure this and my overstrained state. This was a frightful blow to Francis and to me, but after I'd settled down and been in bed for a week I really rather enjoyed it. Everything seemed to go on just the same, and it rather looked as though I was fated to have this enforced rest. Meanwhile Francis had a fall and a leg injury he is still suffering from to this day. This is the sort of thing that happens when you embark on these great projects, but the show must go on.

At the launching of *Gipsy Moth IV* I didn't break the bottle of champagne as successfully as I'd done at the last launching in Ireland, when I simply picked it up and smashed it on the stem. The builder at the yard obviously held the age-old superstition that it's terribly important the bottle should break first time. "Don't throw it, just swing it," he urged me. Marcus Chichester, who was best man at our wedding, also stressed the mystique of the thing: "For God's sake," he said in a dramatic voice, "break the bottle the first time." I began to feel one should have time for a rehearsal, but there was no time for anything—they were in a fuss about the tide and were rushing me. So I swung the bottle according to directions. It came back to me, and so the next time I threw it really hard, and it broke.

Gipsy Moth was very reluctant to go in the water and refused to budge. Francis jumped down and joined the shipwrights and pushed her down the slipway. I felt saddened that those present regarded this as a bad omen. All I was thinking of was that something was the matter with the boat; I could feel it, and so it turned out. She was much too light and 2,400 pounds of lead had to be added to her after the trials. I am quite certain she had a second life; the modifications made after she got to Australia made her more seaworthy though not so fast. But I think only

Francis could have got her there at that speed, she was so unbalanced. I'll never forget the first day I went out on trials with her—she just heeled over and lay on her side. She seemed to prefer sailing that way, and it was really most uncomfortable, to say the least. All that summer we seemed to have rather strong winds in the Solent, a good fresh Force 7, and she was very fast and very wild. I had some hair-raising sails in her with Francis, and at any time I am more nervous sailing there than I ever am in the ocean. There is so little sea room and there are so many big oil tankers using the Solent now.

The changes made after the trials affected my arrangements in the galley, and many of the measurements had to be modified from the way they had been carefully worked out. The comfortable seat we'd been promised got smaller and smaller and ended up as a tiny thing like a bathroom stool for the linen, with a lid and a bit of red foam rubber on top. I believe Francis finally used it to keep his boots in. And there were various other lesser points of the kind which always come up in the frustrations of having a new boat. Then there was the frantic business of finding thousands of pounds by which the estimate had been overrun. Friends came to the rescue, Colonel Whitbread of Whitbreads helped most generously, and this at a time when everybody was cutting down. The International Wool Secretariat, Shell and Ryvita came in with their backing, and at the last minute we persuaded the *Sunday Times* and *Guardian* to be responsible for taking our story—to cope with it technically, I mean. At one time I had thought that if they wouldn't do this, I would take the twice-weekly reports myself and pass them on tapes to the newspapers, but it was a relief not to be burdened with this big chore, and it gave us a nice feeling of support that they were prepared in the end to do it.

It was a terrible storm the night of the final fitting out at Camper's yard. *Gipsy Moth* seemed in a state of chaos, with the Kestrel people trying to fit the set in, men carving the registration number on her, and no-one being helpful about where to put the stores I was trying to get on. The wretched person who comes with the stores is never welcome, and when it's rough and people feel sick, it is even worse. But somehow everything got done, we went ashore for a good dinner, and I spent the night with Charles and Phoebe Blake, two wonderful friends. If it hadn't been for Charles's tact and charm co-ordinating everybody, I don't think the boat would ever have got to sea. As it was, she sailed next morning, and arrived safely at Tower Pier, London.

In spite of the terrible worries we'd been through and the times when everything seemed to going wrong at once, I always felt this world voyage was a great spiritual adventure, a sort of pilgrimage. I had complete faith in Francis's ability to carry it through and never faltered in this.

11

BEFORE we sailed off from Tower Pier to Plymouth, there were two occasions which went off beautifully each in its different way. The first was a Press Conference aboard *Cutty Sark*, organised extremely well by the International Wool Secretariat: an amusing party on a wonderful evening. We came back as the sun was setting, and though Tower Bridge is an ugly structure perhaps, it looked beautiful opening for us that night and gave one a great sense of importance. A few days later we had a moving little dedication service for *Gipsy Moth*. The Harbour Master of the Port of London came and some of our friends and relations, and the Reverend Tubby Clayton—looking very frail, but I thank God he was with us again when Francis returned in July 1967—conducted the service. It was a form of dedication dating back many hundreds of years. Francis read certain passages, I read one prayer and Giles another, and then Tubby Clayton took over. Though I'd had to prepare all this in a great hurry, it was very impressive and I am glad it was done in this way.

At this time also I prepared one of my special prayer cards. In 1960 I had used a prayer card sent to me by Robert B. Laird and I remembered every night the five yachtsmen in the first Solo Race. In 1962 and 1964 I had other ones for Francis which close friends seemed glad to have and use, so this time I had a special card made for his circumnavigation and gave it to about twenty of our friends. On one side was a reproduction of Dürer's Praying Hands, and on the other these prayers:

> O Lord God, when thou givest to thy servants to endeavour any great matter, grant us also to know that it is not the beginning, but the continuing of the same until it be thoroughly finished, which yieldeth the true glory; through him that for the finishing of thy work laid down his life, our Redeemer, Jesus Christ.
>
> Sir Francis Drake 1540-1590

Sheila, Francis and Giles, homecoming, Plymouth, 1962.

The author on board *Gipsy Moth III*, Indian Point, Cape Cod with Cousin Dick and Dudley Clark, 1962.

Sheila launching *Gipsy Moth IV* at Camper & Nicholson's Yard, Gosport, March 1966.

After the dedication of *Gipsy Moth IV* at Tower Pier, London. *Left to right:* Marcus Chichester, Dudley Perkins, Director Gen. P.L.A., Monica Cooper, Commander Gilbert Parmiter, Robin Denniston, Francis, Sheila and Giles, Victoria, Lady Dulverton, the Rev. Tubby Clayton, Paul Hodder-Williams.

O Thou, who sittest above the water floods, and stillest the raging of the sea, accept, we beseech Thee, our supplications for this thy servant Francis Chichester who in yacht *Gipsy Moth IV*, now and hereafter, shall commit his life unto the perils of the deep. In all his ways, enable him truly and Godly to serve Thee, and by his Christian life to set forth Thy glory throughout the earth. Watch over him on his departure and on his landfall, that no evil befall him nor mischief come nigh to hurt his soul and bring Thy comfort to those who wait his safe home-coming. And so through the waves of this troublesome world, and through all the changes and chances of this mortal life, bring him of Thy mercy to the sure Haven of Thine everlasting Kingdom, through Jesus Christ our Lord.

The Old Prayer of the Merchant Navy, seventeenth century,
adapted

By the time Francis came back, literally millions of people were holding him in their thoughts and prayers and wishing him well: this was a tremendous output of power.

The day came to set forth, a very hot one with the temperature soaring to 90°. I was last to come on board and found quite a crowd of friends and photographers there. Colin Mudie came as a fourth member of the crew with Giles and myself; it's not wise to sail short-handed out of the mouth of the Thames with something like a thousand ships a day passing through the Straits of Dover, so that a yacht must look out not to get in their way. *Cutty Sark* waved to us. We were carrying a special pennant she had given us, and away we went, a most glorious sail. I love seeing the land from the sea and Margate, Dover and the white cliffs looked glorious. Colin left us at Newhaven and the three of us sailed on in good weather to Plymouth.

As usual, we had a wonderful welcome. Colonel Whitbread and some of his friends gave us a dinner the night before Francis sailed, and the Royal Western Yacht Club of England had agreed they'd give him a gun. I went out in Mashford's launch to see him off. John and Helen Anderson of the *Guardian* were with us. I remember John leaning over the side holding his head. "What's the matter?" I asked him. "Are you feeling sick?" And the Andersons said, "No, but we're very fond of the old chap." I was amused at this, for it seemed to imply, "There you are standing, all jaunty, and the poor man going off to his death." But Giles and I are used to it; we just said goodbye and Francis went. I cannot explain the strong conviction that keeps me from worrying, being sure of success ahead of time. Or failure, like my hunch that Eric Tabarly wouldn't win the third Solo Trans-Atlantic Race. I don't know why I felt this about Eric, he had a magnificent boat. Yet in fact he did have to put back and was wise not to go on when this new boat proved unready and unsafe. Francis sailed in rough weather and during the few days' rest I took in Cornwall, it was absolutely terrible too. His messages came through the first night, and after that he continued to keep faith with us over 29,600 miles of ocean.

A busy time followed for me, thanking the senders of hundreds of telegrams, writing letters and giving information as best I could. Interest mounted with people reading his story in the *Sunday Times* and getting his position from the *Guardian* in the middle of the week. Already a great following was sailing with him in mind and thought, and it became quite clear to me that I ought to have some further lessons in public speaking. I went back to the Abbey School for Speakers, run by Thelma Seear, who is a brilliant teacher. I asked Lady Joubert to join me, and for six weeks we had a most interesting course at Caxton Hall. Seven men were also students. I owe a great deal to Thelma for what she taught me. One of her mottoes was, "Think clearly to speak clearly."

I tidied up the office, had some hectic moments with various Press people, and looked forward with excitement to my voyage to Sydney to meet Francis. I'd booked a passage on the *Oriana* long before and rather love big liners. Marcus Chichester and various friends sent me off in style, and when I got on board, the Commodore, James Dunkley, came to see me and was charming. To my great surprise and joy, I got a message that I had been given the freedom of the bridge. So when we sailed, there was I on the bridge with all these very smart officers of *Oriana*, and it was thrilling to sweep down Southampton Water and out past the Needles. I thought of the many sails I'd had in yachts, our own and other people's, down these waters I knew so well.

For the whole of this voyage I had news of Francis twice a week. Every afternoon I went up on the bridge and spent time with the navigator while we plotted Francis's course. The whole ship became very interested and we got *Gipsy Moth's* positions in various ways. At Port Said I was able to buy a *Guardian* and read the full edited report. The paper cost five shillings or more and everybody seemed very amused about it, but I said it was well worth the money. As we drew near Australia, the communications men were terribly keen for me to speak from *Oriana* to my husband in his yacht. This had been arranged beforehand; they used to be up half the night trying to get *Gipsy Moth*, but I think they really started before he could be in range. Moreover, the set Francis carried was difficult to get connected with the very different set on a big liner; they didn't seem able to receive him properly, but after various frightful nights of agitation, we finally did speak to each other on November 19. We were over 1,000 miles apart but managed to have a good talk.

Before this there had been one of the crises of this world voyage, and we had shared it though I didn't know the explanation till later. Sitting listening in the radio operator's room, I'd picked Francis up and could hear him saying, "I'm going to Fremantle, I'm going to Fremantle." "Heavens," I thought, "what's happened now?" And the operator said, "Oh my dear, I hope he won't go to Fremantle—that will spoil everything." I felt that way myself, thinking how disappointed Francis would be, and as far as I was concerned, I didn't want to stop off at Fremantle instead of going to Sydney. I hate changing my plans. "Don't let's tell anybody on the ship about this," I said to the radio operator. "Things may change." I went to bed telling myself it was no use worrying and had a good night's sleep. In the morning a note came under the door: "It's all right, he's going on."

What in fact had happened was that Francis's self-steering gear broke. He could not repair it himself and thought he'd have to go to Fremantle to get this done. He had actually set his course and then lay in his bunk and thought and thought until he managed to work out a very ingenious way of making the yacht steer herself. Having rigged up his own contrivance, he set off for Sydney once more. He had expected the original self-steering gear to let him down—the boat was so heavy to steer that the vane just couldn't hold her. In the end it went, and Francis was thankful to get this over. And his own little device worked for the last 2,800 miles sail to Sydney, which was a great feat, for a boat without proper self-steering is tough going for a single-hander.

I arrived in Fremantle to face a barrage from the Press. They insisted on clapping headphones on my head so that they could photograph me as though I was talking to Francis—which of course I wasn't. Then there was a Press Conference. All the same, I should have loved to stay longer in Fremantle, or in Perth, where the black swans are. It is a very coming part of Australia, this, and all is so beautifully planned. They're wonderful people, the Australians, heart-warming in the welcome they give you. On our way to Melbourne, I gave a dinner party to the Commodore, the radio operator, the Press Officer, James McNeish who had been most helpful to me, and the entertainments hostess of *Oriana*. We had a special menu on which our position and the position of *Gipsy Moth* was shown. We were within about four or five hundred miles of each other, not as close as we had hoped when the planning was started over a year before, but I don't think it was bad—a big liner can keep to schedule but it's not so easy for a small yacht, and if Francis had not had this breakdown of his self-steering gear, we should have been even closer.

We called at Melbourne, where I had a charming telegram from Sir Charles Johnston, the British High Commissioner, to welcome me to Australia. When we landed, I found the heat staggering; it was over 100°, and coming out of an air-conditioned ship made it seem worse. Pie Grimwade, who had been one of my tenants at No. 9 in London, met me and took me off to have lunch at her house. I was so overcome by the heat that I asked if I could lie down and have a rest in the afternoon. A frightful storm broke, sweeping down the trees in the garden, and when it was over the temperature fell to about 54°. This is a country of violent opposites. Back on the ship there were more Press waiting for me, an enormous basket of flowers from the editor of a Sydney newspaper, and many people wanting to see me. I found it all a bit confusing.

By the time we reached Sydney, I felt I wanted to land quietly, but the Press Officer said, "Well, I'm afraid our man says you're the person they all want to see, and you'll have to have a Press Conference when you arrive." "I'd much rather do it in the morning," I said. Up on the bridge with the Commodore, I saw *Oriana* brought in and was fascinated at the way this enormous liner was brought alongside, a tricky operation with just the same difficulties as a yacht has. The Press people, instead of waiting to land on a gangway, had become so excited they had come out in the pilot's launch and were on board waiting for me. It was late and I'm never any good at night, but there I was faced with all sorts of questions. I did my best to answer, feeling very tired, and then retired to bed.

A strong wind was blowing as we came into Sydney. If only Francis had had the help of this instead of the head wind he did have all up the coast, he would have arrived much sooner than he did and got nearer his target of a hundred days for the voyage out. But this is just the luck of the draw.

I was met by members of the Australian Wool Board, since the International Wool Secretariat had partly sponsored Francis's voyage. Sir Garfield Barwick, Lord Chief Justice, and his wife Norma looked after me very well when I arrived, keeping in constant touch and helping and advising. Everybody was most kind. Jim Sare from Hodders, Francis's publishers, came along with a charming assistant, Darli McCourt, who was to become a great friend; in fact, I don't know what I should have done without her. Despite this welcome, once I was alone in the apartment I had booked, I must say I felt intensely lonely and missed all the friends I'd made on the ship. But I wasn't to be quiet for long. The telephone kept ringing and there was such tremendous Press interest that I didn't know how to cope.

That Saturday I called on the secretary of the Royal Sydney Yacht Squadron who had offered Francis a mooring. There had been other offers, but it was left to me to decide which was the right place to bring him in to, and I felt certain it would be best to make arrangements here. The secretary showed me where *Gipsy Moth* would be tied up and was most helpful all round. I asked my driver to take me to look at churches in Sydney. There was one I liked very much, Christchurch St. Lawrence, and I attended services there throughout my stay. Then the pressures really started. I was bombarded for information, especially by the *Sydney Mirror*. The representative of the *Sunday Times* and *Guardian* was ill and couldn't come to see me, and no-one had clued me up about syndication and how it was in order for the *Sydney Mirror* to publish messages after they'd been published in London, though not, of course, before. In any case, the thing which was uppermost in my mind despite all this badgering was to get in touch with a meteorological officer for weather forecasts and also with the marine communications director. This turned out to be a real headache, for though there were some famous navigators who could have been a great help, they were too modest and quiet to come forward; it's the tougher people who push themselves on you. This dreadful hunting and breakdown of communications just as Francis was coming into harbour was a familiar pattern of my life. After all, I'd had it twice at Ambrose Light vessel and again, but not so much, after the second Solo Trans-Atlantic Race.

I did make a good friend at this difficult time—the part-time telephone operator at the hotel—and Mrs. Darli McCourt from Hodders and her assistant came in as a strong support when I set up an office. I just had to do this with the mail pouring in and all the business of organising Francis's arrival. He was coming along, and soon I was able to speak to him person-to-person on the radio/telephone. The morning after our first talk, I was horrified to open a daily paper and see printed verbatim my conversation with my husband. "Mrs. Chichester's call," it said, "was monitored by a ham." I rang up Sydney Marine Communications to protest, and my contact there said he was frightfully upset over this infringement of privacy and that of course they would never use a ham to monitor their calls. The next time I spoke to Francis I was dying to say, "All right, boys, I know you're listening and I'm grateful for your interest, but please don't give what we've said to the papers." I heard afterwards that some amateurs are willing to give information to the Press, though it's a fact that when you are given a licence as a ham, you have to sign a declaration to keep secret what you pick up. It's very serious if this form of communication, which is used for big business all over the world, is no longer to be private. The conversation between Nasser and King Hussein picked up on radio/telephone is another strong case in point. But though serious, it's perhaps inevitable.

Gradually things sorted themselves out. I made a move to a very nice suite in the Belvedere Hotel, which proved more suitable at this particular juncture, and Giles arrived, extremely fortunate to get a place in a B.O.A.C. plane because there was a strike on in London. Their Excellencies The Governor General and Lady Casey, old friends of ours, came up to Sydney and invited us to dinner with them. I did so much hope Francis would come in while they were there, but he didn't have enough wind and was delayed. So Giles and I went to this wonderful dinner at Admiralty House where Lord Casey drank Francis's health. Though I was sad he wasn't there with us, it gave me pleasure that Giles was able to meet all these charming people and see his father so honoured.

Some agitating cables arrived from England: Michael Cudlipp of the *Sunday Times* warning me I'd be guilty of a breach of contract if I gave away to a newspaper anything Francis had said to me. Thinking over this whole story now, what strikes me as the most interesting thing is that the word 'positions' never came into any of these newspaper sponsoring arrangements; the agreement was that Francis should send dispatches. I'm afraid it was I who started up all the interest in his positions which became such a fashion and led to fierce battles over them, but I think it has to happen in this age of modern communications. In the Solo Trans-Atlantic Race of 1968, Jan de Kat's life was literally saved because the last thing he was able to do was to give a position which an aeroplane, 37,000 feet overhead, picked up. So ships and planes were guided to the spot, otherwise I don't think he would ever have been found.

I cabled the *Sunday Times* that they really must send someone out to help me, and in the end Murray Sayle arrived to represent them. He was exhausted from a frightful flight because of the strike and the strain of getting planes while other people are left behind, but the Press have to do these things. Meanwhile the Wool Board in conjunction with the International Wool Secretariat agreed to organise a Press conference. The Billiard Room at the Royal Sydney Yacht Squadron was most kindly loaned for what I was told was one of the biggest Press conferences Australia had ever seen. There were some two hundred representatives, and of course they all arrived with lights and cameras and so on two or three days before Francis came in. His batteries were getting low, communications had broken down, and one way and another it was a period of dreadful uncertainty. I was never free of the telephone. Luckily Giles was there to take over many things for me and was very good indeed. By Sunday the whole of Sydney was waiting for Francis, cameras all set up on the South Head to catch his coming in, but he didn't appear.

The Press kept urging me to say something. What could I say? That evening I was called to the telephone at the Sydney Yacht Club: a message from Francis saying he wouldn't be in until the following morning, and that he was sorry to keep everybody waiting.

Next day, in glorious weather, I took a car out to the lighthouse on South Head and talked to Mr. Jolly, the keeper, a most delightful man who had been in sailing ships in his time. He said he hadn't seen *Gipsy Moth* in his long-range telescope, which took in ten miles. There was a report that Francis would be in by one o'clock, that he was off Botany Bay. "He won't be in till five," said Mr. Jolly. And Mr. Jolly was right. Francis had given a police launch an E.T.A. of 01.00 when they said he had only twelve miles to go. When he looked at the chart later he found it was twenty miles against both wind and current. Back at the Yacht Club all was tension, the Press people waiting and waiting, and the yachtsmen who had meant to meet Francis having to go back to work, though a few went out when the time came at last.

Francis appeared round the South Head, sailing beautifully, as he always does. The boat was white and shining, the sails in impeccable order as he always keeps them, and *Gipsy Moth* looked splendid. Though she is such a tricky boat to sail and a nasty character, none of this shows at all. I am always sorry for a yacht when it comes thousands of miles and is caught and put under tow. To me it's rather like a wonderful galloping horse being haltered and dragged along, and this is just what *Gipsy Moth* looked like. She charged about under tow and I thought we were going to be run down in our launch. Then the doctor got on aboard, and I followed, and Giles, and Murray Sayle of the *Sunday Times*. Usually I take the helm when we go out and come in from these ventures; however, there was a delightful Australian water policeman and I asked him if he'd like to take the helm. "Oh yes," he said, "I'd feel part of history." And I was very glad to hand over to him and retire below and give Francis a glass of champagne.

So there it was. To me there will never be another moment like this landing, or another Press Conference like this one. The crowds were so great that Francis and Giles and the *Sunday Times* man disappeared, I got lost and had to battle my way through to get into the Conference, described by Francis in *Gipsy Moth*

Circles The World. It was a very good one, and it was extraordinary later, watching it on television, how he seemed to come to life with these people. Tired though he was, having had no sleep for two nights, he really answered some good questions and everybody was happy. Next morning at the hotel we were woken up by Press people trying to take pictures, and from then on our privacy seemed to go.

Long before I met Francis at South Head, my stepson George had gone out and greeted him. We had arranged this the evening before, when George and his bride, Gay, Giles and myself had had a wonderful reunion. It was very sad that George died so young, in 1967. He had always been delicate, but this was a great shock to us all. I was thankful he and Francis had had this meeting at sea and that George and Gay came to see us again before the end of this Australian visit. Because of George's decision to come out to New Zealand and Australia, he had never met Giles—there was twenty years between them—and since I'd brought up George from the age of eleven, I felt this was a long-delayed family gathering.

Francis has written in his own book of the consultations he had on making *Gipsy Moth* more manoeuverable. Even after certain modifications had been made, the experts still said they didn't feel happy about the boat. There was also frightful pressure from home, everyone cabling us to say, "You've done so well, don't go on." The dangers of the Horn were blown up to frightful dimensions—partly, I think, because Francis had picked out for *Along the Clipper Way*, an exciting guide to his venture, some of the more terrible things that had happened to people rounding the Horn. And it can be very bad weather there at certain times, but it can be calm. There was a general atmosphere of "Prepare to meet thy doom" type of warning, and I had hundreds of letters and some very nasty Press at home, which surprised me. I have come to the conclusion that the world is more full of No-people than Yes-people, and for some reason the No ones wanted to stop him. But he had no idea of stopping, and I'd never even thought of it. This was a project, he was half way.

It never entered my head to worry. I was at my usual job of doing the stores and determined they were going to be well done. Going through everything that had come off the boat, and listing, was a week's job with two girls helping me to check and cross-index. I have never received anywhere such wonderful efficiency and co-operation as I had from David Jones, the store in Sydney which undertook all the packing. We had a wonderful break in the midst of all this hard work when we accepted invitations to stay at Government House and with the High Commissioner at Canberra. On the way there, James Fairfax invited us to stay at his country house which was one of the nicest houses I saw in Australia, beautifully furnished, with a most delightful garden. James also has a very fine collection of Australian paintings. Art there is very, very marvellous and strong, like their characters. At Canberra there was a big Press conference to which I was invited despite being a woman. During question time, the representative of a Russian paper, *Tass*, stood up and asked Francis where he found such a wonderful wife to help him. This was a new question and extremely nice of him. The old one cropped up, of course, why I was never worried, and to this I simply answered: "I am in a very curious position; I am not worried, and yet everybody expects me to be." On a visit to Sir Charles Johnston and his delightful Russian wife, Natasha, we met Godfrey Winn and I had a most interesting talk with him. Later that year he was to do a piece for *Woman* and made me his "Woman of the Year"; I felt very honoured and grateful. The only other magazine interview I gave was to *Nova*.

Back at Sydney, there was still the barrage of Don't and You'll-be-drowneds, comments about setting off at the worst time of the month and so on and so forth. There were also arrangements to be made with newspapers for this second part of Francis's story. The *Guardian* had to drop out for financial reasons, which was sad, but after some delays, the *Sunday Times* cabled "With you all the way," and the *Times* came in and took on the weekly side of the story.

A week before Francis was sailing, on the Sunday, the heat was intense—100° in the cabin—and what with people all over the boat coiling ropes, tidying up, attending to the radio/telephone, and my own efforts to get the stores in, I thought I was going to pass out. The air conditioning at the hotel broke down and I'd dropped into an exhausted sleep beside a fan in another room when the telephone rang. I leapt up to answer it, for I was dying to go out on trials of *Gipsy Moth* with Warwick Hood and Francis, and somehow my right foot, which had gone completely dead while I'd been curled up, gave way beneath me with a nasty click. I had torn a ligament and was laid up for about three days with this injury, which was maddening, though it wasn't a bad thing for me to have this rest. We had made some very warm friends—no-one knows how to entertain as the Australians do— and after Giles had had to say goodbye and go back to Oxford, Robert Anderson, Lady Dulverton's godson, stepped in and helped in every possible way. So did his mother, Lorna Anderson, and of course Darli McCourt was still being a splendid support.

Francis had planned to sail on Sunday morning, January 29. The Friday night before, about ten o'clock, when we were in bed half-asleep, the telephone rang. "Don't answer it," I said to Francis, but he said he thought he'd better. It was Charlie Johnston, and I heard Francis say, "Oh Charlie, it must be all your doing." "Whatever's happened?" I asked him. And he told me Charlie had rung up to say, "You've been knighted." We both felt absolutely stunned; we had no idea this was going to happen and it was the biggest surprise we have ever had. We almost wondered if we were dreaming. But at three o'clock the telephone rang once more, and it was the night porter with a message from the *Daily Mirror* in London who had called up with the same news. It was dreadful being wakened up again, but I told the porter he'd better bring us some tea, though it still seemed like the middle of the night. After we had had this, Francis tackled some of the autograph books which had piled up. We had been loaded with so many wonderful gifts too that there was chaos in the room.

Next morning in the midst of incessant congratulations, we went down to *Gipsy Moth*. I was walking with a stick, my foot all strapped up. Lord and Lady Casey were coming to see the yacht this Saturday evening, and he arrived with a message from the Queen in his pocket. She had sent a special telegram for Lord Casey to bring, and of course we have this still. It was a very wonderful and exciting moment.

We had got the boat as ready as we could, but Alan Payne, the designer of the 12-metre *Gretel*, was still worried about the forward hatch. He didn't think it was fastened strongly enough, and he was right. If there had been time to reinforce it with the timber he'd brought, this hatch wouldn't have opened when Francis capsized three days later and things would not have been so bad for him. But he was due to sail at eleven that Sunday morning and we always believe in sailing on the dot when we've said we are going to—this is part of being a trained ocean racer. So I got in *Gipsy Moth* and took over the helm and away we went, with all kinds of people wishing us luck and being marvellous to us. With us sailed two champagne buckets we had forgotten to return—at the last minute I'd asked for some ice. So when we visited Australia in the Spring of '67, we presented one back to the Yacht Club, with an inscription of where it had been and what it had done. And I think they were quite pleased.

It was coming up pretty rough when Francis left the Heads. They had to go into the lee of the North Head to get me off with my shaky leg, and I still don't know how I managed it, even with help. Other friends on board went outside with *Gipsy Moth*, and they got all the sails up, but it was a job. They couldn't get a dinghy alongside, but finally somebody brought a rubber one and they jumped down into it. I remember there was a glamorous girl in a bikini aboard it, which all added to the excitement. They came back and joined us. Francis sailed away and I felt perfectly confident that all would be well.

12

THERE was only once on this Sydney-Plymouth voyage of Francis's when I was really worried, and that was not for more than three months after this.

It was bad luck that within a few hours of his going very rough weather came up. A real stinking southerly arrived; a lot of boats were capsized and dismasted in some regattas. Within a few hours, Francis had all sails down, and hardly made any progress. When he radioed Sydney with a message he said I wasn't to be given till morning, that he'd capsized but required no assistance, I took this calmly and accepted what he had said. It was 7 a.m. when I got this word, no-one had picked it up, and I told only my host and hostess, Hugh and Bar Eaton. Francis had said that his radio might be damaged, so it was marvellous when he came through that night and gave me the story: what had happened, what he had lost, and that he was all right, the boat had come up again. Personally, I think he was sucked right back in an enormous wave and he was hanging upside down in it as it broke. Had it crashed on top of him, I think he would have been pretty badly off. As it was, it says a lot for *Gipsy Moth's* stout rigging and masts that they were all right when he came up, and for the radio, which continued to work. We talked for an hour and he was in good heart. About twenty minutes later, the *Sydney Telegraph* was on to me, saying there had been a news-flash from London that Francis had capsized. I assured them I'd just been talking to my husband and that all was well, but of course next day there were enormous headlines: CAPSIZE—GIPSY MOTH, and all that kind of thing. *The Times* had this dispatch first, as they were entitled to do, and then released it through the proper channels.

I stayed another week in Sydney, hectically busy coping with telegrams and mail—there were 1,250 communications from children alone—and then after a terrific send-off from Kingsford Smith airport, I flew to Hong Kong. It looked fabulously beautiful as we landed. I had had some rest and peace on the flight, and I stayed now with an old friend, Harry Stanley, who gave me just the quiet time I needed to pull myself together.

The morning after Francis's near-capsize in *Gipsy Moth* on the night of Monday, January 30, the P. and O. liner S.S. *Himalaya*, a very big ship, came into Sydney and reported having been hit by a gigantic wave and knocked to starboard. She was on her way from Wellington to Sydney. While I was in Hong Kong *Himalaya* came in and I asked Harry Stanley if he would take me down to visit the Captain. The Captain called in his chief radio officer. "There is something here I know will interest you," he said. The officer told me how he was on watch at midnight when he heard *Gipsy Moth* calling, speaking to Sydney Radio. When he heard the word "capsize" he immediately took a recording of the conversation which he played to me, and I must say it was very interesting to hear Francis's voice loud and clear and cheerful. The *Himalaya* had thought he might possibly require help, but as he had said "I do not require any assistance", after a conference they went on their way. They very kindly gave me a copy of the ship's storm log that night. The maximum roll recorded was 23 degrees to starboard and 12 to port, and the stabilizer fins were acting at the time. They recorded very, very rough seas indeed and they were taking water to windward and over all. I feel pretty certain that this was the same giant wave that had knocked *Gipsy Moth* and that the liner and yacht were quite close to one another at the time. The Tasman Sea is famous for these confused rough seas and big waves.

A week later I landed at London airport. Then the worst time started for me. Not being worried about Francis, but worried by the pressures from all sides and the way this great spiritual adventure threatened to become dreadfully material, with talk of how we ought to make our fortune, how Francis should be built up into very big publicity, how this one or that one should handle it. But I tried to keep my course on what I knew my husband would like.

About a month before Francis got near the Horn, Captain Cook of the Admiralty told me *Protector* was going down there to meet him. *Protector* is a destroyer on fishery protection and gives information about icebergs. I fought and argued about this plan for weeks, quite sure that Francis wouldn't want anything of it. But Captain Cook was being inundated by Press people and finally agreed to take five of them. I couldn't think why these competing newspapers shouldn't have one representative to feed news to all the others, but this was not satisfactory to them. And in fact I should think these five had a lot of fun in Punto Arenas watching for Francis, who was all the time sending his twice-weekly reports.

So often in my life I have had help and guidance just at the right moment, and in this matter of Francis's rounding the Horn and all the publicity hullabaloo which I hadn't foreseen, I had behind me the advice of Fred Cumber, a wise businessman I met in Hong Kong. The following April I visited him in Gloucester-shire; he was now more or less retired and leading a quieter life farming. He was a lay reader also. When I told him of all these problems with sponsors and Press pressures, he said to me, "You've got a clear course here. Either you do go in for this vast publicity or you pull away from it and do your best to damp it down. It's your choice." Well, money is not a major goal in life. Friends and work and good health really mean far more than having a lot of wealth if it brings you a lot of worry. These terrific business propositions which were afoot were something we couldn't handle, even if we wanted to, without engaging a much bigger staff and transforming the whole enterprise into something quite different. So I made every effort to cut out as much of it as I could, and I knew Francis would feel as I did. During this time, Edward Montagu gave me most generous help and advice on Press relations. I also had a letter from Brother Mandus telling me that he was undergirding Francis's voyage with prayer and had suddenly picked me up on his prayer circuit and had realised there was a close spiritual connection. He came to see me, I had a very uplifting talk with him, and the result of this talk was given in the form of an interview in his magazine *Power Lines* which goes all over the world.

About this time I had a call from the Palace and the Queen's Press Officer, Sir Richard Colville, made a private visit to discuss the knighting of my husband. The Queen was thinking of coming to Plymouth for this. When I mentioned to Sir Richard that we planned to sail up the river and finish at Tower Pier, "If you're sure you are going to do that," he said, "this is the answer." Presently he came back to tell me that the Queen felt that the

Palace of Greenwich would be a suitable place for the investiture. I was sure that, after three months alone at sea, it would have been a terrific strain on Francis for the knighting ceremony to take place almost as soon as he landed at Plymouth. All this was to be kept private until the Palace announced it, which wasn't easy when the Remembrancer, Sir Paul Davie, approached me saying the City of London wished to welcome Francis and give a luncheon in his honour. They wondered why I said he must first stop off at Woolwich. The Chief Harbour Master of the Port of London, Commander Parmiter, had to know what was happening, I felt, and so, with Sir Richard's permission, I told him.

Planning for all this in detail was something after my own heart, and I remember particularly one lovely day when I went down the Thames in the Harbour Master's launch, the *Nore*, with Commander Parmiter, Errol Bruce, and John Fox of Whitbreads, looked at everything and discussed details with an eye to this occasion. The plans worked out between Commander Parmiter and Commander Errol Bruce turned out splendidly in the event. The Navy, of course, are wonderful at organising such things; they have got a long know-how from the past.

On my birthday, April 11, Francis completed his circumnavigation by crossing his outward track in the South Atlantic. I was able to send him a message from London, and though *Gipsy Moth* was 5,000 miles away, the technicians clearly heard his message to me. From then on we were in touch with *Gipsy Moth* up to Plymouth, a remarkable feat of communication for a small yacht. On that day I went to a lunch party with Harold Evans, Editor of the *Sunday Times* and his Managing Editor. This meeting was intended to be a help to everyone concerned with Francis's arrival. From my experience of trying to home him into Sydney, I had an idea how interest was going to mount, though I don't think anybody at the time could have foreseen what the excitement was going to be like when he reached Plymouth.

Soon he would be getting near the Azores, and I told the Editor of the *Sunday Times* that this would be a danger point, that probably people would try to take pictures from the air and rival newspapers to find him, and that I did want him left alone. If anyone doubts I was right, there is no need to look further than Francis's own log entry about *Protector* on March 22: "It was that warship and all the telephoning which fagged me. After 50

128

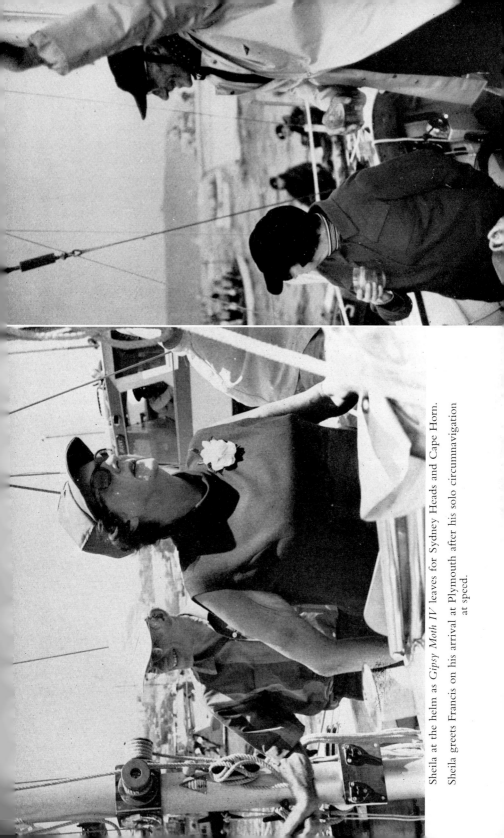

Sheila at the helm as *Gipsy Moth IV* leaves for Sydney Heads and Cape Horn.

Sheila greets Francis on his arrival at Plymouth after his solo circumnavigation at speed.

In the Channel before being met by the Queen at Greenwich.

Gipsy Moth IV arrives at Greenwich Pier.

days plodding across the Southern Ocean alone, I needed the Horn to myself somehow. . . 50 days' solitude is strong medicine." When I heard that the *Sunday Times* was sending a yacht, *Sea Huntress*, to find Francis, get a picture and speak to him, I knew it would be the last thing he wanted. I said they should ask his permission, that I saw no reason to chase him when there was good person-to-person contact from London, and that they must tell me what he said. "He doesn't want us to go particularly," the reporter admitted when she rang up after she had talked to Francis, "but in the end he agreed." They didn't tell me *Sea Huntress* was also taking people from the B.B.C. who were going to make a film and a recording.

When I found this out suddenly, I was distracted about the whole thing—the intrusion on his privacy, the danger that he could be run down, for you can't keep watch all the time when you're sailing single-handed. I pictured them chasing him along when he was tired. He had got trouble with his arm, and as long ago as 1962, when I had discussed this question with him, we'd agreed that sending a dispatch to a newspaper is a very different thing from being interviewed when you are at sea. You are very vulnerable and when everybody is listening it can be acutely embarrassing. I immediately asked Marconi Marine not to give *Sea Huntress* a matching radio set to *Gipsy Moth's*, because I knew that through that they would find him. Marconi agreed, so *Sea Huntress* had to go without this.

To add to the upsets and misunderstandings over all this, I arrived at Brent terminal one evening to speak to my husband on the radio/telephone and found a whole team of television people inside wanting to televise me talking to Francis. This had been arranged, I was told, because it was thought I would like the publicity. How wrong you can be about people! I asked them to go, and finally they went; after that, by order of the Postmaster General, no-one was allowed in there without a pass. Francis told me he didn't want *Sea Huntress* to come, and who finally gave them his position I never found out. I had agreed with the *Sunday Times* to have a code, but I suspect my calls may have been monitored as my calls into Sydney had been. Anyway, they found him, and to my horror on Sunday evening I heard his voice on the tape. He spoke on the News, and also there was a film made which showed him very tired and moving about like a monkey because of his damaged leg and arm, obviously thinking he was out of range of the camera with *Sea Huntress* a mile away.

Later, Dr. Michael Winstanley, M.P., took this whole matter up, saying it was a great intrusion on the last days of this great man's voyage. Mentally I couldn't help dividing my friends into the sensitives and the insensitives—the ones who understood why I didn't want this to happen, and the ones who rushed round and said how marvellous it was to have seen him. I had always accepted the fact that he was bound to be met when he got near the Western Approaches and that there would be hunting for him then, as there was at Sydney.

When *Gipsy Moth* was nearing her goal, remembering how she had been rammed by a launch with enthusiastic Press people on board when she was approaching Sydney, I wrote to all the leading newspaper editors, the I.T.N. and the B.B.C. asking them not to send out boats to hunt for Francis until he was close to Plymouth. I had some very nice letters back from them, assuring me that they understood the dangers of this. I knew quite well that Francis would want to be left alone until he had finished his voyage. When he came in and the gun sounded on Plymouth breakwater, he would have done his part, and that was that. But I had never expected interest to mount as it did, never expected to be forced to withhold his positions, never expected this volume of publicity. In the end, after frightful pressure on me, I just faded out. For about three days he was escorted into Plymouth by the Navy and Air Force, landing late on Sunday evening, May 28.

Francis's was a spontaneous arrival, not stage-managed in any way. Frankly I felt a little embarrassed at keeping the Commander-in-Chief waiting and all the Press—I was told there were hundreds of them there, to say nothing of the colossal crowds which packed Plymouth. The Lord Mayor told me afterwards that half a million visitors had come. But you can't change Francis and he wished to sail in in his own way. He said that if he had known there was such a crowd waiting for him, he would have tried to go faster, but I don't think he could have done, because the wind wasn't there.

In the matter of his homecoming, he, as ever—and I have been married to him for thirty years—really dictated the situation and we had to fall in. As it turned out, *Gipsy Moth*'s arrival was extremely beautiful. I shall never forget how Francis came in just as night was falling, the yacht appeared towards the break-water surrounded by a fleet of other boats. We had the three guns given by Jack Odling-Smee of the Royal Western Yacht Club, who had gone out in his yacht to do this for Francis. The sky was superb with the sun just setting this lovely late evening. It was all sheer excitement but I was beyond that, beyond feeling. Francis called out for sea room, rounded up into the wind and stopped *Gipsy Moth* dead. Giles and I were in the Commander-in-Chief's launch, laden with as many people as we could take. We got on board. I don't really remember what I first said to him. We just met naturally, I had felt so in touch with him all along. I know Francis said, "It's terrible, I don't feel anything," and I said I didn't either. At a moment like that you can't, though people expect you to be all emotional.

Then we had the Marines around us and suddenly it became very thrilling. We broke the traditional champagne and had that. Francis looked well to me, but thin; people always do when they come off the sea. He didn't mention his painful arm, we weren't bothering about details like that. He'd done it, done what I had always expected him to do, and I was completely happy. He had achieved what he set out to achieve: a solo navigation at speed with only one stop and an average of 131 per day over 29,600 miles. I felt tired physically and mentally and knew what lay ahead—the Press Conference, the Lord Mayor's reception, the volume of the crowds which was going to be a shock to Francis. We came in very calmly. There was a mooring waiting for him at the Royal Western Yacht Club's mooring steps. The Queen's Harbour Master came alongside and was the first to give Francis official greeting. It was an awful business trying to get Francis off, finding clothes and the little personal things he wanted. I am told it was a long wait while we were having a mad hunt for this and that, but when someone has come 16,000 miles in a boat, it's not easy. By then there were bonfires and fireworks, a fabulous scene.

We drew alongside and there was the Lord Mayor in his red robes and feathers on his mayoral hat, and he and the Town Clerk greeted Francis. He seemed quite steady on his legs; the last bit up from the Azores he hadn't had much rough weather, whereas when he came into Sydney he was quite exhausted from the strange waters and frightful currents he fought against getting in. We walked through the cheering crowds to a magnificent Rolls Royce. I got in the back with Francis, Giles got in the front, and as we proceeded through the packed crowds they seemed to me like a big solid swarm of bees. I remember thinking, supposing they didn't like you—how frightening it must be if you are a dictator and the crowds turn on you. You could be killed in a moment. The Mayor took us into the Town Hall and after some refreshment we went into the Press Conference. It was nothing like as dramatic as the one in Sydney; by now it was so late the first line men were telephoning their stories to their newspapers, and Francis was asked endless questions about the voyage, many of which seemed to me quite irrelevant, although I have realised since that people were naturally very interested. After a very, very late dinner at Astor House, I felt absolutely exhausted and said I was going to bed. Francis and Giles stayed talking.

Next day passed quietly and Francis seemed in pretty good form. On Wednesday we walked in procession from the Mayor's Parlour through the cheering crowds to a very impressive Thanksgiving Service, the church fuller, I should think, than ever it had been before. Then a visit to the Guildhall, and the Town Hall, where a blare of trumpets greeted us and eight hundred people were there. The Lord Mayor made the most delightful speech. When I congratulated him later he said, "Well, I spent all day preparing it." Which didn't surprise me; it's the case with all good speeches, and even Churchill spent all day if necessary preparing one. You have to take trouble and eliminate; it's like life, it's what you leave out that counts. The reception was very exciting; Francis was surrounded by as many friends and well-wishers as could get near him in the hall. All a bit exhausting, but after a short rest we went to a dinner party for forty people, and at midnight we were photographed with the Lord and Lady Mayoress standing beneath the portrait of Sir Francis Drake which hangs in the Mayor's room. On Thursday the Flag Officers of the Royal Western Yacht Club gave a delightful champagne lunch at a country house for us—and so it went on until Monday.

We went over then to Mashford's Yard, again a great welcome. But when we got on board *Gipsy Moth* Francis suddenly said he felt very faint and tired and must lie down. After a while he felt better, but he told me he must escape, must get away. Enormous pressures had been put on him in these few days, and I don't think any of us quite understood the state of exhaustion he was in. We went up to the beautiful promontory which looks down on Plymouth and had a sandwich lunch there, but still Francis seemed very unwell. I urged him not to go to dinner with the Commander-in-Chief that evening, but he insisted he must when they were having this dinner for us. When I borrowed a thermometer—which I had to do very discreetly, not wanting any stories of illness to be put around—I found his temperature normal, though he had a very, very rapid pulse.

During dinner he suddenly got up and went out with Lady Talbot. I followed, but once he had lain down he said he'd be all right when he had had a rest. After a while I went back, putting as good a face on it as I could, and in fact I was not frightfully worried: there seemed every reason for Francis's tiredness. Twenty minutes later I told the Admiral I'd like to go up and see how he was. The room was empty, night had fallen, and there was no sign of Francis on the bed. I looked down and there he lay on the floor beside it, looking very, very grey and cold. I immediately did all I could to revive him and got him back on the bed. A young doctor arrived and said he couldn't find anything radically wrong; Francis's heart was normal and his blood pressure that of a young man. Lady Talbot told me an ambulance was waiting to take him to hospital, but I took the responsibility of having them drive us back to Astor House instead. Francis was too weak to walk upstairs there, and his arm was hurting him very much. Another doctor examined him but said the same thing as the first. Finally he got off to sleep. The two orderlies who had come to help me seemed thrilled to be looking after him. As they stood by, so kind and calm, I saw them as typical of so many quiet, good people who never get written up.

In the morning the doctor told me my husband could get up for lunch, which amazed me because in my opinion he had really been very ill. In the afternoon, he was taken off for a blood test and an X-ray of his elbow, and the next report was that they found him very low and in need of a blood transfusion. I said I didn't believe in transfusions at all except in the case of a serious accident, but Francis seemed to agree to it and after dinner went to hospital, where they said they'd just keep him for the night and no-one need know.

Next morning I was told he was having a haemorrhage and that they thought he had a duodenal ulcer. This was confirmed. "I've good news," the doctor said. "It's just a duodenal ulcer." Later on he explained that they all thought Francis had cancer again. Extraordinary, this fear. While he was in hospital, I stayed at the Admiral's house, and neither Admiral Miles nor his wife could have been more considerate and kind. They were also wonderful people at the hospital, and though I don't agree with the use of drugs and conventional methods, the nursing is what counts. Something very much on my mind, of course, when Francis went into hospital was the arrangement for the Queen to receive him at Greenwich on June 13. With only a few days left, I took the decision of telephoning the Palace to tell them he wouldn't be well enough to go, and they were most understanding.

Francis was so happy and peaceful in this hospital that although medically speaking he could have left within ten days, he asked whether he might continue his convalescence there. He did this, and we had a very quiet time together, except when I had to go up to London to see to some business problems in the office. If people had more rest in their lives, I am quite sure they would save themselves a lot of ill-health later and probably live longer, but no-one seems to have the will-power to remove themselves from their normal routine even for a short time. This rest was forced on us both, and here again I feel there was a guiding hand in these events.

The day came when all that we had arranged long before could be carried out. The Queen graciously said she would come to Greenwich on July 7, and the postponed luncheon with the Lord Mayor of London was fixed up too. Knowing how busy all these people were, it seemed dreadful to have had to change these plans so much. However, on Sunday, July 2, we left Plymouth as quietly as we possibly could, with just a few boats escorting us, and we really had one of the most wonderful sails I've ever had to London. At my suggestion we stopped for one night at New-haven. I was quite surprised Francis and Giles didn't insist on going on, and at first I rather wished myself that we had, there was such a crush of people the minute we got there and such a cla-mour for autographs. I remember one woman with a child in her arms who said, "Oh do sign for my baby. He'll value it when he grows up." But quite quickly the Harbour Master and other officials came on the scene and we were moved to another berth where we stayed quietly till morning. Off Dover a lot of Press boats came out and went along with us, and the Warden of the Cinque Ports sent a telegram to greet us. Then we had a most lovely peaceful night off the Downs where the old clipper ships used to tie up. Only one ghostly boat came out towards us and when we denied we were *Gipsy Moth* they went away, though they told me later they hadn't been deceived. Another stop next day at the mouth of the Thames—not a soul in sight, absolute peace and quiet. It is only in a boat one gets this peace, and how one values it!

Our first assignment was to meet Commander Parmiter at nine o'clock at Sea Reach Buoy. It was the most marvellous English weather that day and we proceeded up the river to a quite fantastic welcome from the crowds. The children were wildly enthusiastic, the Mayor of Southend came out in his launch and gave us two splendid Cups, one for me as well as one for Francis, which was a very nice thought. They let off some guns at Southend too—a bit shattering but a great welcome. I shall always remember too how we were entertained on the training ship *Worcester*, where we had lunch and waited for the tide. Sir Richard Colville called on us there and told Francis that the Queen had decided to give him the accolade in public. This was the first we knew of it—originally it had been planned to take place in the Admiral President's room at the Naval College at Greenwich—and Sir Richard gave instructions as to what Francis was to do.

That night was spent at the mooring which had been prepared for us off Woolwich, with an early start in the morning because we had to be at Greenwich at ten twenty-five. We were absolutely spot on, Commander Parmiter met us again, and exactly on ten-thirty we drew alongside on the special pontoon put out for us with a red carpet on it, the first, I should think, that's ever been laid for a small yacht in the Thames. And there we saw the Queen standing at the head of the steps, looking very wonderful in a white dress, with the Duke of Edinburgh and the Admiral President. We got off and walked down the long pontoon, which was lined by the Queen's Watermen in their magnificent scarlet and gold uniform. Crowds of people thronged Greenwich and all along the banks. It was all immensely impressive but also very simple.

Francis went forward first on his own to meet the Queen, and then Giles and I. The Queen knighted Francis by the Watergate of the Royal Naval College, using the sword with which her ancestor Queen Elizabeth I knighted Sir Francis Drake aboard his ship at Deptford following Drake's own historic circumnavigation.

Later on I was to have an absolute barrage of criticism in the press for wearing my trouser suit but at the time I was quite oblivious of all this. After a passage from Plymouth, with five nights afloat, you feel quite a swaying movement; I was conscious of this, and Francis said he felt the same. One of my greatest joys was to see there Hester Norris, my mother's maid-companion who looked after her until she died, then came to me and was so helpful looking after us on our honeymoon. She had been very ill and had recovered through prayer and other help. It was marvellous to see her sitting there, and after the Queen left we had a talk.

It was a wonderful moment when the Queen and Prince Philip came on the yacht. I was fascinated by the Queen's beauty and grace and sensitivity and she seemed to be enjoying this occasion. I think we all felt in a sort of gala mood that day, and though we were not supposed to be going back to the Naval College with the Queen and Prince Philip, they invited us to do this, giving us the chance first to talk to our friends. Then it was time to move away to Tower Pier, and by now it was a very hot day indeed, so that I began to wish I had had my trouser suit made in linen rather than in jersey, which normally is ideal for sailing. I was glad of the protection given me from the blazing sun by the scarf-hat which Simone Mirman had given me.

At Tower Pier, the Lord Mayor, Sir Robert Bellinger, was standing with his elegant Belgian wife. In a white Rolls Royce, with two policemen on white horses riding beside us, we drove slowly through the City of London. It seemed to me like a fairy tale. They had planned this to happen in the lunch hour, and enormous crowds rushed out to join those already in place to see Francis arriving. He was very thrilled and excited. On the balcony at Mansion House, Sir Robert presented Francis with a beautiful plaque they'd had made, inspired by one I had seen of Sir Francis Drake's circumnavigation. I am told there were five thousand people in the crowd below and that this exceeded their wildest dreams; certainly I had never seen anything anywhere to match this. When I was asked to choose between Guildhall and Mansion House for this occasion, I chose Mansion House because I thought it more intimate and attractive, and they had backed this choice because there is more space in front of it for people to come, and every inch of this was needed. The banquet again was like a fairy tale: beautiful lifebuoys made of red and white carnations, the Squadron colours—everything so exciting and so right.

After this we drove to our home in St. James's Place. I'd somehow managed to get most of it done up while Francis was away, thinking it would be nice for him to come back to. There were flags all across the street and it was marvellous. Because of the crowds and because Francis had hurt his leg, it wouldn't have been possible for us to walk back from Mansion House, which had been our original conception of the thing, to round off the project begun by his walking from the heart of London where we live and work to Tower Pier, getting on the boat and sailing from there. But everything else had worked out according to the plans I had made with the Harbour Master of the Port of London. Prince Philip remarked that morning: "Yesterday the tide was right out and this pontoon wouldn't have reached." I said, "I know, I had awful thoughts of our arriving and lying on our side," and being a sailing man he could see the joke.

Next morning we went down to St. Catherine's Dock for an exhibition in a special pavilion near where *Gipsy Moth* was anchored. The *Sunday Times* had organised a competition for children during the world voyage and Francis presented the prizes. We had received thousands of letters from children and it was really good to meet some of them there. The first prize was a model of the yacht.

Gipsy Moth went to her home mooring on September 17, 1967 which is also Francis's birthday. Edward and Belinda Montagu organised the most wonderful welcome for us. We came up the river in the daylight escorted by other craft and *Gipsy Moth* was moored just opposite the jetty; we came off in a launch and were greeted by the Montagus. Edward drove us in his Silver Ghost Rolls Royce up to the Bucklers Hard Maritime Museum, where Francis presented him with the charts of his circumnavigation. We then went to a marvellous reception in a marquee, and

Francis was presented with a most beautiful globe of the world in Waterford glass, given him by Francis Showering on behalf of the Mooring Holders of Beaulieu River. As night fell, the Soho Concertente under the direction of Nicholas Jackson gave us a concert in the open air. They played Handel's Water Music and the Royal Fireworks Music. *Gipsy Moth* was floodlit, there was a magnificent firework display with five thousand people present, and all this created a deep impression. The yacht was well and truly home, for this is where we have had a mooring for the past fourteen years, and now Edward has given it to Francis for life. It was wonderful to be among all our friends, Bill Grindey the Harbour Master, Mr. and Mrs. Martin of the shop and other kind people who have looked after us so well.

From the time *Gipsy Moth* arrived back in Plymouth, there was debate about her future. In the end, this was arranged very quickly. At the Boat Show in January 1968 Lord Dulverton formally presented the yacht to London, entrusting her to the Cutty Sark Society to exhibit at Greenwich. We owe this to Mr. Frank Carr, the former Director of the Greenwich Maritime Museum; it was his energy and faith that got her organised to go to Greenwich in the face of many difficulties and much opposition. Mr. Desmond Plummer, on behalf of the Greater London Council, gave the site in the Cutty Sark garden where *Gipsy Moth* will remain permanently beside that great clipper of the past. Between the two of them, they drew capacity crowds. From July 10, 1968, when she was opened to the public at her new berth, up to May 26, 1969, 137,151 people have visited *Gipsy Moth*. On Whit Monday 1969 alone there were 1,474 visitors. The proceeds go to the Cutty Sark Society, but part of those from *Gipsy Moth* are devoted to Lord Dulverton's Youth Centre at Lochiel in Scotland, where boys are trained in adventure, sailing, mountaineering and so on: it is a wonderful place for them. I like to think of *Gipsy Moth* as the children's boat, for during Francis's voyage, which such a multitude of people shared through his dispatches, the children most of all were the ones who seemed to pick up and understand the whole thing thoroughly. People now say that *Gipsy Moth* has gone to her final rest—I think this is a good thing because she really was a rather dangerous boat, and if she had been sailed by anyone who was not extremely expert, heaven knows where she would have landed up.

I think that in life if you go forward you seem to find the right people to work with, people with the same aims. For example, it was Sir Geoffrey Cox who persuaded me, in the end, to help I.T.V., who proved delightful people, and I was very pleased when they got the prize for their news story of *Gipsy Moth* coming into Plymouth. Then there was a print of *Gipsy Moth* called "Horn Abeam", in which I was involved with a well-known art dealer in Bond Street. This became a 1966/67 best seller. I had no idea that out of a project like this sort of Francis's, so much commercialism would spring up. I believe quite a lot of money has been made out of it by the sale of various souvenirs, but it hasn't been made by us. We are, at the time of writing, just breaking even, I believe, on certain products which I monitored myself to avoid anything in bad taste bearing his name being sold. Despite heavy copyright and patent fees and lawyers' fees, I would think a small income will come in from these products. What has done well is Francis's book *Gipsy Moth Circles the World. The Lonely Sea and the Sky* had a big circulation, and I think his anthology with a commentary, *Along the Clipper Way*, was something one could read with the utmost fascination as he made his voyage. I read it then myself and saw how he had prepared it as a guide to what he set out to achieve, part of his very carefully thought out circumnavigation. But the *Gipsy Moth* book was the culmination of a great story, and the publisher came right behind us, everybody working at fantastic speed to get it out for Christmas.

The global interest in the story was caused by the communication, though very few people seem to have realised this. I am pleased Francis has been awarded the Medal of Honour by the Veteran Wireless Operators of New York, and like to remember how Scotty Hamilton, supervisor of Sydney Marine Radio, told me he'd written to congratulate Marconi Marine on their Kestrel set. "But," he said, "I think most congratulation goes to Sir Francis and that he is a natural radio operator, although he was quite untrained." Francis seemed to work up everyone's excitement as he went along, and I think his description of rounding the Horn was brilliant. This story grew and grew, followed by the whole world, and it was a break through in modern communications.

By doing a thing thoroughly—and by thoroughly I mean

paying attention to detail—you get wonderful results in life. If there's one inevitable law, it is the law of returns, and this voyage of Francis's, planned and co-ordinated by brilliant people who helped to make it the success it was, does seem to me a true instance of "casting your bread on the waters". In the chapter I contributed to my husband's book, I quoted Claude Muncaster's letter in which he said that the venture had a very great significance: "A significant illustration of the power of thought coming from thousands and thousands of people, not just well wishing. That happens anyway. This is another, greater power—the power of prayer, if you like, although people don't know about it as such, has gone out as a sort of protection. He has been surrounded by a protective envelope of power." I said then that this put my feeling into words far better than I could express them, and it does so still.

13

I VERY much admire simplicity and I think that as you grow more mature, this is certainly something to aim at. Your clothes should be simple and right, and your food, your possessions and your way of life. Though the modern world is complex and noisy and frightening in being so cut off from natural things, there are moves towards simplification which are very good. Fashion is an example, and sailing, and art. A well-dressed woman has a few dresses in her wardrobe which are right, a well-rigged yacht has a few sails in her locker which are right, a really good picture can have just a few lines if they are the right ones.

I think modern fashions are wonderful: the Grecian styles, the natural styles, the comfort of clothes without padding out and constriction, the shoes which are being designed today to the shape of the foot, so that young people will not have the misshapen feet their mothers possibly had. But women are very strange. They always seem to be obsessed with having one very unnatural thing. We have had very tight waists (the Victorian crinolines were very charming but it must have been bad for the wearers to have their waists so pulled in); we have had terribly pointed toes, frightfully high heels and those extraordinary bustles they wore around 1900. Then there was a phase—I remember my mother and aunts adopting this fashion when I was a child—of having boned collars round the neck. Like the bound feet in China which stopped the women running away, these were signs of woman being prisoner to the male. Today you would have thought we'd had an entire break through, starting with the shingled hair, short skirts and Chanel dresses in the twenties. At the age of eighty, this remarkable woman is still designing clothes that women like. It is a fallacy that men know how to dress women; they dress women in the way they like to see them and don't study what the women feel like. The particular oddity of the later 1960s is false hair. Most of this trade comes through Hong Kong, it's making enormous fortunes for people who sell hair, and the resulting styles are beautiful but unnatural. Hats—which most of the young have never worn—have been pushed to one side by all these gigantic hair-do's. Long ago in my mother's day, to wear a hat for lunch was a kind of fashion symbol, and all women in that generation used to appear at a lunch party in a hat. I think that, in general, a hat should be functional and comfortable, nice to have on your head to keep you warm, or dry, or to stop your hair blowing about, and that, like a man, you should be able to leave it in the cloakroom of a restaurant when you go to lunch. Hats for evening wear—almost in the category of headdress—are very attractive, and I think this fashion is coming back now. Even bows on the hair are pretty; all these things add a glamour and finish to a woman's appearance. At the "Women of the Year" Lunch last year, we were asked to wear hats at the top table, though the young girls didn't, and were very charming with their long fair hair. Lady Lothian, for instance, wore a big turquoise blue hat with the kind of brim that does something for you, and she looked absolutely enchanting in it. For sailing I have had some very good caps designed for me by James Wedge.

Dispensing with handbags, or at any rate not clinging to them on public occasions, is another of my personal campaigns against clutter. Business women can carry a brief-case—I think there's a big market for someone who can design a good business woman's brief-case-cum-handbag, two pieces of luggage in one. And I have at last got over the difficulty of getting adequate pockets put in my trousers, wherever I want them, so that I can carry my key and what money I need quite safely. Tailors just tend to lay it down that ladies don't have pockets in their trousers, and it is all too easy to be weak and give in to this. I did so myself at one time, but now my dressmaker copes beautifully. Another case where there's still room for improvement—there are signs of it, but we are still very far behind the Americans—is designing modern, comfortable bathing suits for women past the age when bikini and bra are becoming. We still cling here to that awful old-fashioned, rather shapeless thing which pulls people into the shape of a tree trunk: a sort of garment with the legs cut off. I designed a bathing suit which was made up for me in 1964 and was much admired at Bailey's Beach in America because it was original and different, a three piece in black stretch jersey bound with turquoise, with a look of the 1920s. You want something you can get into easily, zipping up the front, and none of those terrible struggles that go on under flapping tents or in the open on British beaches.

Air travel has brought about the biggest change in fashion. When I went to Paris as a girl, we had to wrap up with very heavy, thick clothes, the boats were draughty and hanging about in the Customs absolutely freezing. Today you can go away to New York as easily as if you were going away for the weekend in the old days, more easily, probably. You can have a very simple wardrobe, clothes of light fabrics, very practical and attractive, drip-dry things, and for extra warmth one of those feather-light quilted nylon coats. The couture lined clothes of the past, the heavy, stiffened coats that are right out of date now, are no loss whatever; today's fashion, simpler in every way, appeals to me enormously.

In the sailing world, too, there has been tremendous simplification which is good in itself and a great advantage to yachts-women. It was a great move forward when yachts went on to synthetic sails. I remember persuading Francis to have the first one we had because it was so light. Only some eighteen years ago, when we started sailing in the early '50s, most yachts had canvas sails, heavy and holding the damp, and you read of the terrible suffering of the men in clipper days handling frozen sheets and sails. When I saw the huge spate of canvas trousers, skirts and dresses, I always thought to myself that these must surely be made up of material originally meant for sails and not being used for that purpose any more. The number of sails has also been greatly cut down. When *Gretel* came over from Australia, I was told she had dozens of sails in her locker. In 1964 I asked the designer of the winning *Constellation* how many sails he had. "Eight, and I am hoping to eliminate one of these," he replied. I found this fascinating.

It is not awfully easy to get the simple, basic food I feel sure is right, especially as you grow more mature. The young do need building up and it is only after twenty-five or so that people can start to put on weight and lose their figures. The growing trend of keeping thinner and eating less is tied up with the social conditions of today; partly economic, I think, and partly a global conscience. Knowing as much as we do about starvation and over-

143

population in the world, there is this tendency to feel we mustn't eat too much or be too big and take up too much room. And that is in the interests of health. If you eat too much, you are going to get ill or you are going to get too fat. People who have lived to a great age weren't necessarily vegetarians but do seem to have lived frugally, taken exercise, and not indulged themselves too much. Since I became interested and really very closely connected with the vegetarian world, which after all has been going on for thousands of years, I have noticed how many poets, artists, musicians and writers are vegetarian, or turn to it.

When I was a child, we did eat rather a lot. I was forced to, and long before that horrible meat we had at school, I can remember being made to sit in front of my bacon in the nursery until eleven o'clock in the morning because I wouldn't eat it. We did, of course, take a great deal of exercise then, and people don't today, though the papers are full of exercises you can do as a substitute for the simpler thing of walking to the office or at lunchtime. I believe two miles' walk is the minimum you can do to keep yourself fit, and that the big meals eaten in the past by people who rode a lot and worked manually and really used their bodies are right out for the way we live today. Meals have been simplified and courses cut down, but there's still the problem of all these packaged, doctored things. Fish, of course, has not been injected or tampered with in any way, but most of the animals people eat have been so treated that they are far from their natural state. Caponised chickens, battery hens and so on fill me with horror, but that is the way things are going. I think you should have proper wholemeal bread which you can now get all over England—there is an enormous trade growing up for it; natural foods like honey, dried fruits, vegetables, salads. Something I should certainly have invested in if I had had any money at the time is 'Plantmilk Limited', milk scientifically made from grass instead of this cruel business of getting a cow in calf, taking the calf from it and using the milk as human food. This factory also produces the most wonderful chocolate made from this milk, and I think that this pure and compact nourishment could and should help many starving peoples in the world.

I believe in fasting. This clears up many conditions and is really so logical. If you have eaten too much or tired your body out, it needs rest. People have their cars serviced, look

The Queen welcoming
Sheila at the Watergate,
Greenwich.

Sir Robert and Lady
Bellinger, Lord Mayor
and Lady Mayoress of
London, and Lord Simon's
grandson at Tower Pier
7th July, 1967.

Sheila escorted by Admiral of the Fleet, Earl Mountbatten of Burma, at a banquet in the Painted Hall of the Royal Naval College, Greenwich to commemorate Sir Francis receiving the accolade.

after their animals and so on, but they often forget to look after their bodies, though these are almost as important as their minds and spirits. Just live on water and fruit juices and you will lose weight, but you will feel wonderful. Fasting definitely increases your sensitivity and clears your mind. Some people even do it if they want to hear music better. I've never done any very long fasts—six days is the longest I have gone without food—but my husband and I regularly take a day off or a weekend off and just fast. It's only the first day that is difficult, and after that you really don't want to eat. The results are very rewarding, but of course you have got to understand it. It is curious how fasting is probably a psychological thing. During my first fast—quite a long one—I was nervous and had the most blinding headache for a while. Now I feel both well and happy doing it. One must return to eating very slowly, but this comes naturally because you really feel quite reluctant to begin taking solid food again.

When you are young it is quite impossible to imagine being old, let alone dying, but we must all pass along this road. Very few people seem to face up to the certainty of death or read about it, as I have done. Looking at people's deaths, it seems to me the Moslem way is best; to fast towards the end so that you leave your body without any violent struggle, just quietly. It must be better to die in a natural way if you can. I think that in many ways a death at sea would be preferable to most others, if you take only yourself into account. Out once in a big storm with Francis, I was frightened, but not at the thought of dying. I was frightened for my young son, Giles, at home in England, and thought I had been wrong in making this Atlantic crossing in *Gipsy Moth* after the Solo Race. I suppose most mothers must feel like this. Many people have said to me that it is the manner of death which is frightening, but you don't remember being born and therefore when you die I don't see there is anything to fear. Death comes in many ways, some very strange. When Annie Besant, the founder of Christian Science, died, the doctors said she was the most physically perfect woman they had ever examined at death: the clock stopped, that was all. These things are very mysterious, and I think they should be kept in mind. I don't consider this morbid; it is the modern attitude of going through life ignoring the inevitable end of it which is wrong.

All mechanical means of communication—printing, radio,

television, television communications of every kind—are rushing ahead, always in the news and an overpowering influence in today's world. Communication between human beings, between the Church and laity, hospitals and doctors and their patients, man and God, can't be seen progressing in anything like the same way. Here I must say how much improvement I think there could be if women, who have a natural gift for understanding and sympathy, were given more chance of acting as communicators, the role they play in promoting a happy life within the home. With more women to help them, communication between priests and their congregation would be quite different. Almoners do a wonderful job in hospitals, taking time to listen to people and realise their problems. Women could do a great deal more in Trade Unions and in any number of other places where better communication would be to everyone's advantage. Probably all this will come. Men as the dominating sex have called the tune for hundreds of years, expecting women to understand *them*. Nowadays the balance is changing, and they are beginning to realise, almost too much, that women are getting control of affairs. Even the youngest of secretaries in London, flitting round like butterflies, are seen as indispensable assets.

But to go back to the revolutionary new means of communication, the type I have been so involved in has been the instant reporting of my husband in situ from the ocean. I wonder what the old sailors would have thought, what Sir Francis Drake would have thought of someone rounding the Horn three centuries later, describing his feelings and the conditions as he passed it and these being flashed to the world? There was something very wonderful about this shared experience. The other side to it is the overwhelming public interest which can have a terrible effect: the vast crowds to greet a man as unaccustomed to this as my husband and extra-sensitive from months alone at sea, for long ocean passages do produce in you a very natural, open state; the determination of the Press to get a story—any story—connected with the hero of the moment (in Australia even what my husband ate for breakfast was considered newsworthy); the pestering of anyone connected with him to answer questions on the telephone, to be interviewed for freelance articles and exposed to the constant risk of being tripped up and saying something unwary. With top Press men it is easier, but even so they can be ruthless in getting things out of you and you have got to sharpen your wits. Above all, on television, interviewers show no mercy; they are trained people and you are not. In the end I think the public will rebel at watching men and women being stuck on a screen and pilloried, probed and turned inside out.

On the other side of the picture, good, reliable journalists are useful members of society: Anne Sharpley, for instance, who is for ever studying social problems and bringing them before the public in excellent articles. And for great reporters I have nothing but admiration, men like Alistair Cooke, or the late Ed Morrow and Richard Dimbleby, who started these big television interviews co-ordinating people at great distances. Men such as these are communicators on a very big scale—the nerve centre between two or three personalities—and these programmes done nowadays in a global fashion bring us all very close in an impressive and rather frightening way, working on the whole for good. Language difficulties, the necessity for an interpreter which must have given a turn for the worse to many conferences between Heads of State, are unimportant where you are dealing with clear visual impressions. Learning things through the eyes is an easy method to me and to many other people who find it takes them a great deal of concentration to learn through the written word. On television today we do get an opening up of the doors of social conscience, revelations as shocking as the pictures of Van Gogh were in the nineteenth century when he painted, for instance, the sufferings of miners in Belgium, and took for subjects peasants and humble men and women, where before only kings, cardinals, princes, marshals and queens had been thought worthy of a portrait.

Some people say that carrying radios on yachts has taken the romance out of sailing. From a life-saving angle, however, radio sets are wonderful, and in the Sydney-Hobart race, for instance, where it is obligatory for each yacht to carry a set and give its position, it's all made much more exciting for the public—rather like watching race-horses, for though the race goes on for some time, you can follow the contenders from day to day. For planes to go out hunting a yacht blind, without positions, is a terrible waste of money, even allowing that this sort of live operation is useful as a training. There is no reason why the Solo Atlantic Race shouldn't have air coverage; if our people went out their

1,500 miles and the rest was covered by the Canadian Air Force, it would be very interesting. In my opinion competitors should be obliged to carry radios. If enough lone, dreamy ones want to do the voyage without them, realising it will be sheer and extreme good luck for them to be found should they get into difficulties with their position unknown, then they could go off at their own risk, give no reports and have a nice sail. Two races, one with radios and one without, might be an idea.

I don't think it will be long before dinghy races across the Atlantic are possible. This may sound laughable, but think of Manry's achievement or the fantastic passage made in that tiny boat, *The Egg*. As modern radio communication develops, there is no reason why dinghies shouldn't have the support it can give. Before the Trans-Atlantic Race started, I admit I had the idea that anyone carrying a radio/telephone might be very handicapped because of the work involved. Eric Tabarly's broke down in 1964, and in fact he told me he'd never meant to use it. Francis used his, and I worked out that the time taken in charging it, writing despatches and so on, would take him up to two hours a day. That would come to two and a half days on a total passage of thirty days, quite a consideration. But Geoffrey Williams, the brilliant young Cornishman who won the 1968 Race in splendid fashion, proved me wrong. He had a very interesting and up-to-date method of control. The weather report given daily by Bracknell, our meteorological centre, was rushed by car to London where the forecast was fed into a computer, plus the position —latitude and longitude—which Williams sent daily by radio/telephone. The computer gouged out the choice of three courses he could take the next day. His win was a technical triumph, and with lighter radios, single side bands, dry batteries to eliminate the charging problem and so on, there is no reason why boats much smaller than Geoffrey Williams's or even *Gipsy Moth III* shouldn't have all the assistance they want, though of course they would still have to rely on their own decisions which could only be made on the spot.

All this is technical, of course, and I may be sticking my neck out. On simple human communications, as between one person and another, I feel on surer ground. It has a two-way system: you must be receptive, have sympathy and understanding, before you can help anyone. And you must try to help them in the way they want to be helped. I get a lot of letters from people whose loved ones are ill. It is no good trying to impose on them what you think is right. You have to listen to them and then decide how it might be best to meet their needs. This calls for a great deal of sensitivity and it also takes time. The pity is that doctors don't have time to listen to people, and that in hospitals especially, very few have the right approach in what they say to the patient or his family. Either they speak almost as though they were addressing another doctor, in terms which can't be clear to the ordinary, untrained person, or they just don't seem to understand that you are an intelligent human being and no fool, even under the stress of fear or pain. It is the Ward Sisters who show up as marvellous people, and the women who do the actual nursing. As for experimental operations on human beings, heart and kidney transplants and publicity about them, the sooner the medical profession learns to perform them in decent privacy, the better. Bad communication between doctor and patient, in hospital and elsewhere, brings a vast amount of unnecessary suffering. A great friend of mine, a leading psychotherapist, has told me he spends his days sitting listening to people and their troubles, often people who haven't been listened to when they were children. I do think you have to be very careful when you have children around, doing your best to give them of your time and not to rush them. When they have newly come into the world, they seem to me to be in another dimension; young children are much more sensitive than adults and don't want to be hurried.

It is fairly rare to meet someone with whom you immediately feel in tune; I never know quite why this happens. Some people say it is a level of sensitivity—you seem to understand each other at once and have pleasure in each other's company. Then, again, you meet people you feel you'd never reach any understanding with in a hundred years. I have noticed that in any walk of life, it is those people who commit themselves and above all are true to themselves—whether they are atheists, Roman Catholics, or of any other persuasion—who command respect and seem to have grown mature. Far too many people are not positive enough, and you must be positive in your beliefs to be helpful, even while you have to try to see other points of view as well.

I believe that God is everywhere and in everyone. On one

occasion I was getting on to a bus in the King's Road, Chelsea, laden with my painting materials and feeling very exhausted (it was Christmas time, everybody rushing and a bit tired), and the conductor spoke to me so crossly and gave me such a push I nearly fell over. He harangued all the wretched passengers, going for them the whole way to Green Park where I made a move to get off. The conductor was still shouting at people when another man came down from the upper deck and turned to him and said, "Are your feet bad, mate?" This passenger had such a kind look on his face, I glanced down at the conductor's feet and they were the most terrible I have ever seen. I felt ashamed of the thoughts I'd had about him, while someone else had gone straight to the reason for his bad temper. Just one bus conductor can make or mar hundreds of people's day. Many of them are wonderful the way they cope with the rush hour and keep their sense of humour, managing the sort of smile that gives you a lift; I suppose it is a question of goodness coming through. Bad communication, anger and fear or a few cross words, can affect a whole household or put out a whole office. We all live so closely with each other, are so connected. You can be harmed by words, or you can be blessed by them, every word is registered in the atmosphere—we know it can be picked up on television and all these mechanical devices. I think this is a very important thing to remember. The principle of loving your neighbour is a very high one and terribly difficult to live up to. Francis firmly believes in the power of witch doctors and evil influences, and certainly there seems something in it.

I remember one day suddenly beginning to look at older people, really noticing them. An old gentleman was crossing the road in St. James's Street; I felt very sorry for him and started to realise how it would be in old age. When I meet a really crippled person or someone obviously ill, I always put up a little prayer for them, out of the feeling I want to help them. I firmly believe prayer is an output of power if it is used in the right way, made for an individual and the whole group of human beings to which they belong. Prayer does grow and grow. I saw this extraordinary growth when millions of people were watching my husband on television during his world voyage and praying for him. It all started—I looked at my list only yesterday—with the twenty people who had my personal prayer card. One of the prayers used at the Dedication Service just before Francis left Tower Pier, the adaptation from the old Merchant Navy prayer which I have quoted, was used during his circumnavigation in quite a few churches, notably in the Chapel of the House of St. Barnabas in Soho. John Hester remembered Francis every week. The prayer was used also in our own church of St. James's, Piccadilly. Only recently when I opened a fête in Little Compton, Gloucestershire, the vicar told me they had prayed for Francis very regularly there. I shall never know how many congregations and how many individuals held him in their thoughts before God, but it is clear that a great number of people believe as I do in the power of prayer, or they would not have done this,

All people are healers if they did know it and if they could use this gift for good. Certainly people who are closely in touch with the Creator, either by prayer or meditation, or just being still, are able to transmit to others these powers of healing and peace. I greatly admire, for instance, the Franciscan Brothers at Cerne Abbas. You meet these men who seem completely natural, not particularly worldly nor yet particularly priggish, and they seem to have the right answers to your questions and be able to give them with suitable simplicity. In the same way, at sea one feels this closeness to the Creator and a consciousness of being part of his Creation. During my two Atlantic passages, watching those great seas roll on me, I seemed to feel the rhythm of the world, that this incredible globe we live on was turning and these waters swirling backwards and forwards, drawn by the moon. Undoubtedly people feel more religious at sea, and many people have prayed for the first time, aware of the presence of God. Sailing is a natural life, a sea passage clears your mind of trivialities and at the same time gives you a great capacity for pleasure over small events: dolphins playing in the bow wave, or a turtle swimming past. I have never seen a whale on my voyages and was envious of Giles and Francis when they told me on the radio telephone that they'd just seen two of them in the Atlantic, their backs glistening in the moonlight. Away from the stress of modern life, it is much easier to feel tranquil and happy and make good resolutions, but when you get back into the thick of it keeping these up and keeping calm, in touch with spiritual and non-material things, is very difficult. Saints achieve a special relationship with God through being by themselves and receptive to those unseen powers which we know surround us and which can only readily communicate themselves in solitude. Some who retire from the world are available to us and can give wonderful advice and guidance on a completely uncluttered level. Others who have lived in the world have tried to teach and influence those around them, as Fenelon did the great, the rich and the profligate of Louis XIV's court at Versailles. Trappist nuns and monks who spend their whole time praying for other people and trying to draw nearer to God must be an enormous strength to the world, whether we realise it or not.

Pain and suffering can be a great communicator. I have been told of people who, when they were dying, have spoken to those around them and drawn close to them as they could never have done in their ordinary lives. I believe you must try to know yourself, and through that you are able to try to understand your neighbour; then, finally, strive for closer communication with the Creator. Simplicity to me comes into religion also, and it is some of the ancient prayers thought out in stillness and solitude that seem to me entirely right for today. One of my favourite prayers is St. Augustine's: "Thou hast made us for Thyself and our hearts are restless until they find rest in Thee." In September 1968 the Bishop of Coventry invited me to join his call to mission. I had met him the year before when there was a very impressive service of thanksgiving for Francis in the Cathedral. My theme to speak on was "Living with Purpose", and I tried to explain what religion meant to me, that if you have faith in God you have faith in yourself, and faith in your fellow men and women. I ended by speaking of the restlessness of today which is so well summed up in the words of St. Augustine.

I think we were brought up in my generation to believe what we were told, to accept too much without question. It is very good to try to find out but dangerous to doubt everything or to think that a super-scientific and material approach will solve all mysteries. God will reveal when we are ready. My biggest search in life has been the search for truth and to find God, and I shall go on with this to the end of my days.

INDEX

Abbatt, Lindley, 87, 88
Abbey School for Speakers, 114
Abyssinia, 31, 33;
  Emperor of, 34
Addis Ababa, 33, 40
Aden, 33, 34
Agra, 32
Aitken, Sir Max, 99
Ajmer, 31
Alcoa Pointer, 95
Along the Clipper Way, 121, 139
Ambrose Light vessel, 88, 91–2, 93,
  101, 102, 118
America, 39, 71, 72, 88–95, 100–4, 106
Anderson, Helen, 113
Anderson, John, 100, 113–14
Anderson, Lorna, 123
Anderson, Robert, 123
Arklow, 84
Astor House, 132, 133
Atlantic Ocean, 128;
  Solo Races, 10, 70–2, 77, 82, 86–7,
    147–8,
    (1960) 86–94, 112,
    (1964) 105–6,
    (1968) 88, 106, 114, 119, 148;
  Sir Francis's Record Crossing,
    100–2, 105;
  Sheila's crossings, 94–9, 103–6, 145,
    151;
  Giles' crossings, 106, 151;
  dinghy races, 148
Australia, 12, 35, 43, 124, 143
  during circumnavigation, 9, 109,
    115–24, 146
Australian Wool Board, 117, 119
Azores, 94–6, 98, 128, 131

Bailey's Beach, 142

Baker-White, Robin, 40
Bali, 43
Barton, Esme, 33, 34
Barton, Lady, 34
Barton, Sir Sidney, 34, 40, 45
Barwick, Sir Garfield, 52–3, 117
Barwick, Lady, 117
Beatles, the, 83
Beatrice, Princess, 15
Beaulieu River, 64, 86, 138
Becton Gas Works, 46
Belle Eau Park, 13
Belle Ile, 65
Bellinger, Sir Robert, 136
Belvedere Hotel, Sydney, 118
Besant, Annie, 145
Birkenhead, Lord, 57
Biscay, Bay of, 65
Bishop Rock, 105
Blake, Charles and Phoebe, 110–11
Blew Jones, Douglas, 24, 36
Bombay, 32
Bonhame, Muriel, 91, 93
Bordighera, 23
Borneo, 44
Bournemouth, 36
Bovill, Ann, 19, 21
Bracknell, 148
Brasher, Christopher, 91–3
Bremond, Jean, 20
Brent radio terminal, 100–1, 129
Brightlingsea, 57–9
Bristol, 45
Britannia, 57
British Broadcasting Corporation, 97,
  98, 100, 105, 129, 130
Brown, Ulick, 24
Bruce, Commander Erroll, 128
Buckingham Palace, 31

153

Buckler's Hard, 89;
  Maritime Museum at, 137
Bundi, 30
Burma, 46
Burton, Tiny, 79
Bushell, Anthony, 52
Buxey sandbank, 58–9

Cadogan, Mrs., 19
Café Royal, 46
Cairo, 35
Calcutta, 32
Camper's yards, 108
Canary Islands, 24–5
Canberra, 122
Cannes, 23
Cap Horn, 88, 89, 91
Cape Cod, 103
Cape Horn *see* Horn, Cape
Cardigan, Lord, 51
Cardinal Vertue, 89
Carleton, John, 59
Casey, Lady, 118, 123
Casey, Lord, 118–19, 123
Cerne Abbas, Franciscan Brothers of,
  84, 151
Channel Islands Club, 66
Charms, 34
Chelsea, 35, 44–5;
  Old Church, 40
Cherbourg, 63–4, 66
Chichester, Emily, 45
Chichester, Sir Francis,
  knighting of, 9, 123, 127–8, 134–6;
  illnesses of, 10, 68–70, 72–81, 84,
    85, 133–4;
  marriage to Sheila, 24, 36–41;
  charms, 34;
  flying of, 39, 43;
  navigation by, 39, 65–6, 70, 80, 82;
  forestry business of, 43;
  during World War II, 44–8
  buys first boat, 55;
  books written by, 120, 121, 139;
  see also
    Atlantic Ocean, Race
    Gipsy Moth I–IV
    World, circumnavigation

Chichester, Francis Ltd.
Chichester, Francis, Ltd., Map
  and Guide Publishers, 49, 53, 60,
  79–82, 100
Chichester, Gay, 121
Chichester, George, 41–3, 44–5, 46,
  48–9, 121
Chichester, Giles, 86;
  at his father's investiture, 9, 136;
  birth of, 50–2, 82;
  up to age of seven, 53–4, 57, 79;
  education of, 54, 59–60, 75, 94,
    100;
  sailing, 60–2, 65–6, 103–5, 106, 151;
  parents sailing without, 63–4, 68,
    90, 94, 96, 100, 145;
  appendicitis of, 68–9;
  during his father's illness, 75, 77;
  and *Gipsy Moth III*, 85;
  and *Gipsy Moth IV*, 112, 113–14;
  and circumnavigation, 118–21, 123,
    131–2
Chichester, Marcus, 109, 114
Chigwell Row, 45
Christchurch St. Lawrence, 117
Christian Huygens, 44
Circumnavigation of the World
  see World, Circumnavigation of
City Island, 94–5
Church's Council of Healing, 83
Clark, Robert, 69–70
Clayton, Rev. Tubby, 85–6, 100, 112
Colchester, 57, 58
Colthurst, Charles, 58–9
Colville, Sir Richard, 127–8, 135
Communication
  between people, 10, 146, 148–52;
  between man and God, 10, 146,
    152;
  mechanical means of, 12, 139,
    145–7;
  between doctor and patient, 17,
    146, 149;
  between Church and Laity, 146;
  women and, 146;
  the Press and, 147;
  and children, 149
Concarneau, 65–6

Connolly, Ed, 91
Constellation, 143
Cooke, Alistair, 101, 102, 147
Cook, Captain, 126-7
Cooper, Monica, 81
Cornwall, 86, 114
Corunna Race, 62
Coventry, Bishop of, 152
Cowes, 56-7, 70, 87
Cox, Sir Geoffrey, 139
Craven, Sir Charles, 28
Craven, Gerald, father of Sheila Chichester, 13, 16, 26, 37
Craven, Thomas, grandfather of Sheila Chichester, 13, 18-19, 20-1, 23, 25, 28-9 37, 40, 44, 56
Craven, Kathleen *see* Thompson, Kathleen
Craven, Mollie, 40
Craven, Ethel, mother of Sheila Chichester, 13, 16, 18-19, 20-1, 56
    illnesses of, 25, 26-8;
    death of, 27-8, 35, 36, 69
Craven, Nancy, 57
Cudlipp, Michael, 119
Cumber, Fred, 127
Cutty Sark, 112, 113, 138;
    Society, 138

Daily Express, 99, 105
Daily Mirror, 19, 123
Daily Sketch, 91
David, Villiers, 53
Davie, Sir Paul, 128
death, 145
de Kat, Jan, 119
Delhi, 31
Devon, 35, 36, 49, 77;
    see also Plymouth
Dimbleby, Richard, 147
Dimbleby the Spaniel, 48, 52
Dinard, 62, 66;
    Race, 64-5, 68
Djakarta, 43-4
Djibouti, 33-4
doctors, distrust of, 27-8
Douglas Hamilton, Lord Malcolm, 45, 92

Dover, 71, 113, 135;
    Straits of, 113
Drake, Sir Francis, 112, 132, 136, 146
dress designing and making, 20-1, 23-4
Dublin, 85
Dulverton, Lord, 105-7, 138
Dunkirk, 45
Dunkley, James, 114, 116
du Pont family, 103, 106
du Pont, Mrs. Dick, 94
du Pont, Felix, 94, 95
du Pont, Marka, 94, 95
Duvernet, Mlle, 19-20, 22
Dyas, Valerie, 19

Eastbourne, 28
Eaton, Hugh and Bar, 125
Edith G, 92
Edstone, 69
Egg, The, 148
Elizabeth I, Queen, 136
Elizabeth II, Queen, 9, 123, 127, 134-6
Enton Hall, 76
Estoril, 26-7
Everett, George, 98
Evetts, Margaret, 23-4

Fairfax, James, 122
Farria, Claudine, 96
Farria, John, 96
fashion, 141-3
fasting, 144-5
Fastnet Races, 68-9, 70, 85
Fayal, 95, 96
Fenelon, 152
Figaro, 70, 92
Flandres, 89-91
Florence Edith see Gipsy Moth II
food, 143-4
Foster, Clive, 40
Fox, John, 128
France, 23-4, 35, 45, 77-8, 86, 100
Franciscans, 84, 151
Francis Chichester Limited, Map and Guide Publishers, 49, 53, 60, 79-82, 100

Fremantle, 115–16
Fulham Road, 24
Fyfe, Miss, 19

General Post Office, Marine Department, 100, 107
Geoghegan Jack, 10
George V, King, 57
George VI, King, 34
Germany, 44, 45
Gipsy Moth I, 56
Gipsy Moth II, 56, 67, 68–9
Gipsy Moth III, 69, 76, 85–6, 89–99, 101–6, 148
Gipsy Moth IV, 9, 12;
  built, 105–10;
  launched, 109;
  dedicated, 112–13, 150-1;
  leaves Plymouth, 113–14;
  to Australia, 114–24;
  from Australia, 124–32;
  capsizes, 125–6;
  on return to England, 132–8;
  on show at Greenwich, 138;
  print of, 139
Gipsy Moth Circles the World, 120–1, 139
Goodwin, Geoffrey, 43
Gosport, 107, 108
Grand Hotel, Plymouth, 105
Grant, Pauline, 52
Great Barrier Reef, 43
Greater London Council, 138
Greece, 9
Greenwich, 134, 135–6, 138;
  Gipsy Moth IV at, 135–6, 138;
  Maritime Museum at, 138;
  Palace of, 128
  Royal Naval College at, 135–6
Gretel, 123, 143
Grimwade, Pie, 53, 116
Grindey, Bill, 138
Guardian, The, 100–3, 105, 108, 110, 113, 114–15, 117, 122
Guernsey, 62
Guild of Air Pilots and Navigators, 92
Gulf Stream, 95

Hall, Eve, 26
Hamilton, Laurence, 94, 100–3
Hamilton, Scotty, 139
Hamstead, 56
Hannay, John, 80
Harding, Rev. Geoffrey, 83
Hasler, "Blondie", 87, 88, 91
Hatherop Castle, 19
Hayward, Madge, 24, 25
healing, 10, 17, 26, 28, 82–4. 91, 149, 151;
  Church's, Council of, 83
Heavenly Rest, Church of, 91
Helford River, 86
Herne, Rex, 102
Hester, John, 151
Hester, *see* Norris, Hester
Hill, Geraldine, 79
Himalaya, 126
Hodder and Stoughton Ltd., 107, 117, 118
Hong Kong, 125–8, 141
Hood, Warwick, 122
Hore-Ruthven, Sir Alexander, 34–5
Horn, Cape, 121, 126–7, 129, 139, 146
Horstmann, Freddie, 27
Horta, 95–6
Howe, Dr., 83
Howells, Valentine, 88–90
Hughes, Arthur, 44
Hughes, Mrs. Arthur, 45
Hughes, Henry, Navigation Instruments, 44–5
Hulbert, Jack, 35
Humphries, His Honour Judge Christmas, 83

Ilford, 45
Illingworth, Capt. John, 106
Independent Television News, 130, 139
India, 28–9, 30–3, 34, 35
International Wool Secretariat, 110, 112, 117, 119
Ireland, 85

Jellicoe, Lord, 57

Jersey, 63
Jersey, Lord, 15
Jester, 91, 92
Jesuits, 75
John XXII, Pope, 84
Johnson, Amy, 39
Johnston, Sir Charles, 116, 122-3
Johnstone, Lady, 122
Jolly, Mr., 120
Jones, David, 122
Jones, Martin, 85
Joubert, Lady, 114

Kelly, Father, 75
Kennedy, President John F., 101-2, 103
Kensington Palace, 14-15
Kensington Palace Gardens, 21, 29
Kestrel, *see* radio/telephone
Kindersley, Archie, 56, 60
Kindersley, Dick, 56
Kindersley, Edith, 37, 40, 56
Kirklington Hall, 13

Lacombe, Jean, 88, 89, 91
Laird, Robert, B., 112
Lampson, Sir Miles, 35
Land's End, 89, 105
Latto, Dr. Gordon, 76
Laurence, Brother, *The Practice in the Presence of God*, 84
Lewis, Dr. David, 65, 88-9
Little Compton, 151
Lizard Light, 97, 105
Lloyds, 89
London, 10, 12, 20-1, 24-5, 27, 35; City of, 128, 136-7; Lord Mayor of, 134, 136
London, Port of, 70-1, 112, 137
London Man, 81
London School of Domestic Arts, 19
London Woman, 81
Lonely Sea and the Sky, The, 139
Long Island Sound, 102
Loomis, Alf, 91
Lothian, Lady, 142
Louis XIV, King, 152
Lyttleton, Dame Edith, 39

McCourt, Darli, 117, 118, 123
McCullough, Donald, 100
MacEwen, David, 32
McNeish, James, 116
Madras, 30, 32
Maharishi, the, 83
Mait, 85
Manchester, 13
Mandus, Brother, 127
Manning, Harold, 101
Manry, Mr., 148
Mansion House, 136-7
Marconi International Marine Co. Ltd., 100, 107, 129, 139; *see also* radio/telephone
Margate, 113
Marie Fidelia, Sister (Aunt Ella), 15, 17
Martin, Mr. and Mrs., 138
Mary, Queen, 15, 57
Mashford, Syd, 69
Mashford's Yard, 69, 132
Mattei, Dr. Jean, 78
Matthews, Joy, 57, 81
Mauritania, 90
Mayfield, 27
meditation, 26
Melbourne, 116
Mervyn, Sonia, 82
Mieville, Sir Eric, 34
Miles, Admiral, 133-4
Millbay, 98
Miranda, 87, 93, 95
Mirman, Simone, 136
Montagu, Lord, 127, 137-8
Montagu, Lady, 137
Morrow, Ed, 147
Mudie, Colin, 113
Muncaster, Claude, 140
Munich crisis, 45

Nanny, 14, 15
Nantucket, 91, 101
Needles, the, 64, 66, 114
Newbiggin Hall, 41
Newtown River, 56, 58
Newport, U.S.A., 106
New York, 71, 88, 89-96, 101-3, 139, 143;

New York—*contd.*
  Mayor of, 90, 94
New Zealand, 36, 37, 39, 41-3,
  48, 121
Nicol, Stormy, 65-6
Nore, 128
Norris, Hester, 26, 37-8, 39, 40-1,
  136
Northampton General Hospital, 15
Nova, 122

Observer, The, 87-9, 92-3
Odling-Smee, Colonel Jack, 87, 131
Open Way, 83-4
Oriana, 114-16
Ostend, 60-1
Oxford, 13, 123
Oyster, Harbours, 94, 106

Pages, 45-8
painting, 21, 82-3
Paris, 10, 18-23, 82, 143
Paris Match, 102
Parmiter, Commander, 128, 135
Payne, Alan, 123
Percy, Captain Jim, 92-3
Perth, 116
Peshawar, 30-1
Philip, Prince, 99, 135-6, 137
Pflieger, John, 91
Pico, 96
Pink, Dr. Cyril, 51-2, 53, 79, 83, 84
Pink, Marguerite, 83
Plantmilk Limited, 144
Plessen, Victor and Victoria von, 44
Plummer, Desmond, 138
Plymouth, 9, 69, 70, 87-9, 90, 91, 94,
  98, 100, 105, 112, 113, 127-8,
  130-6, 138, 139;
  Commander-in-Chief, 130-1, 133;
  Lord Mayor of, 90, 44, 100, 105,
  130-2
Pollocks Rip, 104
Port Said, 35, 115
Port Sudan, 35
Portugal, 26-7, 35, 96
Power Lines, 127
Practice in the Presence of God, The, 84

prayer, 26, 78, 84, 112-13, 127, 136,
  140, 150-2;
  cards, 112-13, 150-1
Press, the, 9, 39, 41-2, 91-3, 94,
  102-3, 105, 106, 109, 112, 116,
  117, 118, 119-21, 127, 129-32,
  135, 146-7
Protector, 126-7, 128
psychology, 82-43
Punto Arenas, 127

Queen magazine, 9-10
Queen Elizabeth, 103
Queen Mary, 92
radio/telephone, 12, 89, 90, 91, 92,
  100, 103, 110, 115, 116, 118-19,
  122, 128, 129, 139, 145-8

Reardon, Bucky, 70-1
Reilly, Sir Bernard, 33, 34
religion, 18, 53-4, 75, 78, 149-52;
  see also prayer
riding, 30-1, 34
Richey, Mike, 86
Ritz Hotel, 47
Rolfe, Thelma, 81
Royal Drawing Society's silver
  medal, 18
Royal Ocean Racing Club, 62, 64
Robbins, Teddy, 70-2, 92
Royal Sydney Yacht Squadron, 117,
  119, 120, 124
Royal Western Yacht Club of
  England, 87-8, 98, 105, 113, 131,
  132
Royal Yacht Squadron, Cowes, 56-7
Russia, 39
Ryan, Mr., 29
Ryvita, 110

St. Augustine, 152
St. Barnabas, House of, 151
St. Bartholomew, Church of, New
  York, 91
St. Catherine's, 70
St. Catherine's Dock, 9, 137
St. Gabriel's House, 15-16
St. James's, Piccadilly, 151

St. James's Place, 47–50, 52, 53–4, 106, 137, 150
St. Malo, 62, 68
St. Margaret's, Westminster, 20
St. Mark's Gospel, 84
St. Mary's, Wantage, 15–19, 41
St. Paul, France, 77
St. Peter Port, 62–3, 66
San Sebastian race, 65
Sao Jorge, 97
Sare, Jim, 117
Savernake Forest, 51–5, 82
Savoy Hotel group, 80
Sayle, Murray, 119, 120
Scilly Isles, 86
Sea Huntress, 129–30
Seear, Thelma, 114
self-steering device, 87, 93, 95
Shadow Isle, 101–3
Sharpley, Anne, 147
Sheep's Head Bay, 92
Sheep's Head Bay Yacht Club, 93
Sheila Chichester's Shopping and Fashion Guide, 81
Showering, Francis, 138
Southend, 135
Sunday Times, 9, 88, 110, 114, 117, 119, 120, 122, 128, 129, 137
Shell Group of Companies, 110
Sheraton East Hotel, 91, 94, 100
Sibley, John, 103
simplicity, 141–3, 152
Single-handed Solo Atlantic Races, 10, 70–2, 77, 82, 86–7, 147–8; 1960, 86–94, 112; 1964, 105–6; 1968, 88, 106, 114, 119, 148
Sloane Avenue Mansions, 35
Slocum Society, 87, 88, 91
Smeaton, David, 98
Snaith, Bill, 70
Solent, 70, 103, 107, 110
Southampton Water, 112
South Head, Sydney, 119–21
South Kensington, 27
Spain, 35–6
Stanley, Sir George, 32
Stanley, Grisel, 51

Stanley, Harry, 126
Stanley, Rosemary, 30, 32
Staten Island, 101, 102
Steer, George, 46
Stitchcombe, *see* Savernake Forest
Strathaird, 30–1, 32, 34
Sydney, 43
  and circumnavigation, 114–26, 128, 129, 130, 131, 132;
  Hobart race, 147
Sydney Marine Communications, 118
Sydney Marine Radio, 139
Sydney Mirror, 117
Sydney Telegraph, 125

Tabarly, Eric, 105–6, 114, 148
Tack Institute, 79–80
Taj Mahal, 32
Talbot, Lady, 133
Tass, 122
Thames, River, 71, 113, 128, 135
Thompson, Kathleen, Sister of Sheila Chichester, 13–14, 16–18, 22–3, 24, 25, 26, 28–9, 30, 35, 47–8, 49, 64, 99
Thompson, Peter, 40
Thurston, Libbie, grandmother of Sheila Chichester, 14
Thurston, Mary Ann, great-grandmother of Sheila Chichester, 13–15
Tickell, Col. Marston, 66–7, 86
Times, The, 122, 125
Times, New York, 103
Titanic, 15
Torquay, 27–8
Tower Pier, 111, 112, 127, 136, 137, 151
Travis, Caroline, 9
Treasure, Rev. Bertie, 53
Tregoning, Enid (née Branston), 17, 19
trouser suits, 9–10, 136
Tyrrell, John, 85–6

Udaipur, 30
Ushant, 66, 97

vegetarianism, 19, 51, 53, 54, 144

159

Vence, 77–8
Veteran Wireless Operators of New York, 139
Victoria, Queen, 13–14, 15
Victoria and Albert, 57
von Blomberg, Field-Marshal, 44
von Zedlitz, Professor Billie and Mrs. Alice, 42, 43

Ward, Edward, 46
Wedge, James, 142
Weeks, Joy, 100
Weems, Commander, 39
Wellington, New Zealand, 41–3, 126
Westminster School, 59–60, 94, 100
Westward Ho, 35, 36
Whitbread, Colonel, 100, 110, 113
Wiano Yacht Club, 104
Wight, Isle of, 14, 56–7, 70
Williams, Geoffrey, 148
Willingdon, Lady, 31–2, 33
Willingdon, Lord, 32, 34
Winchester, 37
wind vane, 87, 93, 95

Winn, Godfrey, 122
Winstanley, Dr. Michael, 130
Wolf Rock, 105
Woman, 122
"Women of the Year" Lunch, 142
Woodward, Dr., 83
Woodbridge, 55, 62
Woolwich, 135
Worcester, 135
World circumnavigation, by Sir Francis Chichester, 9, 10, 12, 57, 77, 82, 83, 146, 150–1;
first proposed, 106–10;
set out, 113–14;
to Australia, 114–24;
from Australia, 124–40
see also Gipsy Moth IV
World War I, 56
World War II, 43–9
Wren House, 14–15, 21

Yarmouth, 64, 107
Y.M.C.A., 46, 47, 57